The Sovereignt

The Sovereignty of God

ARTHUR W. PINK

REVISED EDITION

THE BANNER OF TRUTH TRUST

THE BANNER OF TRUTH TRUST
3 Murrayfield Road, Edinburgh EH12 6EL
PO Box 621, Carlisle, Pennsylvania 17013, USA

*

☺ I. C. Herendeen
First published 1928
Sixth edition 1959
British revised edition by courtesy
of I. C. Herendeen first published 1961
Reprinted 1968
Reprinted 1972
Reprinted 1976

ISBN 0 85151 133 3

*

Set in 10 on 11pt. Linotype Baskerville
Printed in Great Britain by
Hazell Watson & Viney Ltd
Aylesbury, Bucks

PUBLISHERS' PREFACE

THOUGH Arthur W. Pink was one of the most prolific Christian writers of this century he has left us practically nothing of a personal and biographical nature. In *Studies in the Scriptures*, a monthly magazine which he maintained almost solely by his own pen for thirty years, we catch no more than fleeting glimpses of his various pastorates and wide travels. That he was born in Nottingham in 1886, that he preached his first sermon there about 1908, that he ministered in the United States and in Australia, that he returned to this country in the 1930's and spent the remainder of his life in study and in writing, these are about all the facts that are apparent. An evangelical through and through he was nevertheless content to remain comparatively unknown amongst evangelicals in the land of his birth and he passed away unnoticed by the religious world in the Island of Lewis on July 15, 1952.

The life of A. W. Pink inevitably reminds one of similar instances that are to be found in Church history of men whose work was passed over by their own generation only to be prized by those which followed. For there can be little doubt that the writings of the late A. W. Pink are now becoming more widely known and more highly valued than they were in his own lifetime. This is particularly true in the United States, where many of his works have passed through a number of editions.[1]

The main emphasis of Mr. Pink's written ministry was on Biblical exposition and experimental godliness. Thus

[1] The circulation of A. W. Pink's works in the U.S.A. has been largely due to the initiative and foresight of the *Bible Truth Depot*, Swengel, Pennsylvania, who have made available in book form much of the material which originally appeared in *Studies in the Scriptures*.

in his commentaries and expositions of Scripture characters we often find him at his best. Outstanding in the latter field is his *Life of Elijah*, characterized by a fresh spirituality and a vigorous application of the truth. His work on *The Life of David*, is also a stimulating study. In all his writings he makes use of the work of divines who have gone before but does not hesitate to take an independent line where he feels Scripture warrants it. His commentaries on *The Gospel of John* (3 vols.), on *Hebrews* (3 vols.) and on *The Sermon on the Mount* reveal his reverence for the Word of God and also his practical concern to reach not only the mind, but the heart and conscience of the reader. We find this same experimental emphasis in all Pink's writings—in his lesser works such as *Gleanings in Genesis* and *The Seven Sayings of the Saviour on the Cross*, and even in his more doctrinal writings such as *The Satisfaction of Christ*—a study of the Atonement—and *The Doctrine of Sanctification*. However strongly he insists on the doctrines of Scripture, he never views correct doctrine as an end in itself, but rather as a means to a greater end—the glory of God in the salvation and sanctification of sinners.

In recent years there has been, especially among young evangelical ministers, a marked revival of interest in the subject of this book. Nevertheless it is evident that a great deal of confusion exists about the meaning and implications of the doctrine of Divine Sovereignty. This truth has been so little expounded in the pulpit and so rarely—in this century—explained in print that it is hardly surprising that this should be. It is also understandable in such circumstances how some Christians, having only heard a caricature of the doctrine, are unconsciously prone to reject both the misrepresentation and the truth together.

Before this first British edition was printed, the text of the American edition was carefully read over by several friends and ministers who are familiar with A. W. Pink's works, and who love the truth which he here sets forth. As a result it was unanimously agreed that the contemporary value of the book could be increased by certain minor revisions and abridgements. Although Mrs. A. W. Pink's health is such that she was not personally able to supervise such a revision, she graciously gave her permission for us to adopt this course.

There are two practical matters which it is always well to remember in connection with the doctrine of the sovereignty of God. Firstly, while this is a truth which every minister of the gospel is called to proclaim, it is not a subject which should be made a matter of argument amongst Christians. Indeed, the Christian who professes to believe this truth and yet talks as if others can be persuaded to accept it by the power of words and discussion is, in reality, denying his very profession. The one who truly believes that grace and light and spiritual understanding are gifts of God will not attempt to argue about such matters. Rather he will seek to adorn the doctrine by a quiet and patient spirit and to " put on . . . as the elect of God . . . kindness, humbleness of mind, meekness, longsuffering; forbearing one another, and forgiving one another, if any man have a quarrel against any: even as Christ forgave you, so also do ye " (Col. 3: 12, 13).[1]

Secondly, we need to remember that the only attitude in which we can profitably consider this subject is the attitude of *faith*. We must approach such a theme conscious that " the wisdom of this world is foolishness with God " (1 Cor. 3: 19). Here we are on ground where our thoughts are not God's thoughts nor His ways our ways. Divine Sovereignty is not a truth which we can believe of ourselves; we cannot arrive at it by any process of natural reasoning; we cannot receive it merely by the reading of a book; indeed a man may even read the Bible all his life and yet, if left to his own understanding, never find this truth.

Moreover, we are by nature not only blind to this truth, but such is our fallen state that we are as strongly averse to

[1] There would doubtless be less opposition to the doctrine of Divine Sovereignty if all who professed this truth remembered the example of such English Reformers as Bishop Jewell, to whom one Roman Catholic opponent was forced to exclaim, " In thy faith thou art a heretic, but surely in thy life thou art an angel."

it as were Christ's hearers in Nazareth and beside Galilee long ago.[1] A doctrine so diametrically opposite to the natural pride of the human heart cannot but arouse objections. To all objections there is but one answer and that is the statement of the apostle Paul in Rom. 9:20, omnipotently applied to the heart by the Holy Spirit, " Nay but, O man, who art thou?" Only when we are thus brought to know *ourselves* can we be in a position to learn of God, and when a man learns of Divine Sovereignty in this manner it is a lesson he will never forget throughout eternity. " I can remember well the day and hour," wrote C. H. Spurgeon, " when first I received those truths in my own soul—when they were burned into me, as John Bunyan says—burned as with a hot iron into my soul; and I can recollect how I felt I had grown on a sudden from a babe into a man—that I had made progress in Scriptural knowledge, from having got hold once and for all of the clue of the truth of God."[2] The great Reformer and martyr, William Tyndale, likewise knew of only one way in which the Sovereignty of God could be learnt, " Except thou hast felt thyself brought unto the very brim of desperation, yea, and unto hell-gates thou canst never meddle with the sentence of predestination, without secret wrath and grudging inwardly against God. Therefore must Adam be well mortified and the fleshly mind brought utterly to nought, ere that thou mayest bear with this thing, and drink so strong wine."

As it is only the Holy Spirit who can reveal the Sovereignty of God, it is not surprising that in those ages such as Tyndale's, when the Spirit has been poured out in such an abundant measure, that this truth has been clearly known and loved. The Sovereignty of God is glorious in the eyes of those whom the Spirit has " brought utterly to nought." For centuries, prior to the Reformation, when the Holy Spirit was in great measure withdrawn from the Church, this truth had been buried out of sight. It had been so universally rejected and forgotten that it seemed

---

[1] Luke 4:25-28 and John 6:63-66.
[2] *The Metropolitan Tabernacle Pulpit*, Vol. 7. p. 85.

impossible that it could ever be commonly believed again, yet once the Holy Spirit returned in power to the Church this doctrine immediately sprang to life and thundered forth like a giant suddenly awakened out of sleep. Likewise in our own day, if the Holy Spirit is pleased mightily to revive the Church, then all the efforts of years to silence and pervert this truth will be gloriously overthrown.

Such a book as this must cause serious thought, but it is not intended to provoke mere intellectual discussion. It should drive us to prayer. It should fill us with joy for, as Isaac Watts says,

> " The more Thy glories strike mine eyes
>   The humbler I shall lie;
> Thus, while I sink, my joys shall rise
>   Unmeasurably high."

It should bring more calmness and peace into our daily Christian walk. It should take our eyes off men and fix them on " Jesus the Name High over all, in earth and sea and sky." And it should lead us to look with confident assurance for the coming of that day when heaven shall resound with the shout from a multitude which no man can number, " The kingdoms of this world are become the kingdoms of our Lord, and of his Christ; and he shall reign for ever and ever." (Rev. 11: 15).

The Publishers.
July, 1961.

CONTENTS

INTRODUCTION

IT has often been pointed out that a fundamental require-
ment in expounding the Word of God is the need of *preserving the balance of truth*. With this we are in hearty
accord. Two things are beyond dispute: God is sovereign,
man is responsible. In this book we have sought to expound
the former; in our other works we have frequently pressed
the latter. That there is real danger of over-emphasizing
the one and ignoring the other, we readily admit; and history furnishes numerous examples of both. To emphasize
the sovereignty of God, without also maintaining the ac-
countability of the creature, tends to fatalism; to be so concerned in maintaining the responsibility of man, as to lose
sight of the sovereignty of God, is to exalt the creature and
dishonour the Creator.

Almost all doctrinal error is, really, Truth perverted,
Truth wrongly divided, Truth disproportionately held and
taught. The fairest face on earth, with the most comely fea-
tures, would soon become ugly and unsightly, if one member
continued growing while the others remained undeveloped.
Beauty is, primarily, a matter of proportion. Thus it is with
the Word of God: its beauty and blessedness are best per-
ceived when its manifold wisdom is exhibited in its true pro-
portions. Here is where so many have failed in the past. A
single phase of God's Truth has so impressed this man or
that, that he has concentrated his attention upon it, almost
to the exclusion of everything else. Some portion of God's
Word has been made a " pet doctrine," and often this has
become the distinctive badge of some party. But it is the
duty of each servant of God to " declare all the counsel of
God " (Acts 20: 27).

It is true that in the degenerate days in which our lot is

cast, when on every side man is exalted, and "superman" has become a common expression, there is real need for a special emphasis upon the glorious fact of God's supremacy. The more so where this is expressly denied. Yet even here much wisdom is required, lest our zeal should not be "according to knowledge." The words "meat in due season" should ever be before the servant of God. What is needed, primarily, by one congregation, may not be specifically needed by another. If one is called to labour where Arminian preachers have preceded, the neglected truth of God's sovereignty should be expounded—though with caution and care, lest too much "strong meat" be given to "babes." The example of Christ in John 16:12: "I have yet many things to say unto you, but ye cannot bear them now," must be borne in mind. On the other hand, if I am called to take charge of a distinctly Calvinistic pupil, then the truth of human responsibility (in its many aspects) may be profitably set forth. What the preacher needs to give out is not what his people most like to hear, but what they most need, i.e. those aspects of truth they are least familiar with, or least exhibiting in their walk.

To carry into actual practice what we have inculcated above will, most probably, lay the preacher open to the charge of being a turncoat. But what matters that if he has his Master's approval? He is not called upon to be "consistent" with himself, nor with any rules drawn up by man; his business is to be consistent with Holy Writ. And in Scripture each part or aspect of truth is balanced by another aspect of truth. There are two sides to everything, even to the character of God, for He is "light" (1 John 1:5) as well as "love" (1 John 4:8), and therefore are we called upon to "Behold therefore the goodness and severity of God" (Rom. 11:22). To be all the time preaching on the one to the exclusion of the other, caricatures the Divine character.

When the Son of God became incarnate He came here in "the form of a servant" (Phil. 2:6); nevertheless, in the manger He was "Christ the Lord" (Luke 2:11)! Scripture says, "Bear ye one another's burdens" (Gal. 6:2), yet the

same chapter insists " every man shall bear his own burden "
(Gal. 6: 5). We are enjoined to take " no thought for the
morrow " (Matt. 6: 34), yet " if any provide not for his own,
and specially for those of his own house, he hath denied the
faith, and is worse than an infidel " (1 Tim. 5: 8). No sheep
of Christ's flock can perish (John 10: 28, 29), yet the Christian is bidden to make his " calling and election sure " (2
Peter 1: 10). And so we might go on multiplying illustrations. These things are not contradictions, but complemen-
taries: the one balances the other. Thus, the Scriptures set
forth both the sovereignty of God and the responsibility of
man.

In this present work, however, it is with the Sovereignty
of God that we are concerned, and while the responsibility
of man is readily owned, yet we do not pause on every page
to insist on it; instead, we have sought to stress that side of
the truth which in these days is almost universally neglected. Probably 95 per cent. of the religious literature of
the day is devoted to a setting forth of the duties and obligations of men. The fact is that those who undertake to expound the responsibility of man are the very writers who
have lost " the balance of truth " by ignoring, very largely,
the Sovereignty of God. It is perfectly right to insist on the
responsibility of man, but what of God?—has He no claims,
no rights? A hundred such works as this are needed, ten
thousand sermons would have to be preached throughout
the land on this subject, if the " balance of truth " is to be
regained. The " balance of truth " has been lost, lost
through a disproportionate emphasis being thrown on the
human side, to the minimizing, if not the exclusion, of the
Divine side. We grant that this book is one-sided, for it only
seeks to deal with one side of the truth, and that is, the
neglected side, the Divine side.

THE SOVEREIGNTY OF GOD AND
THE PRESENT DAY

WHO is regulating affairs on this earth today—God, or the Devil? That God reigns supreme in Heaven, is generally conceded; that He does so over this world, is almost universally denied—if not directly, then indirectly. More and more are men, in their philosophisings and theorizings, relegating God to the background. Take the material realm. Not only is it denied that God *created* everything, by personal and direct action, but few believe that He has any immediate concern in *regulating* the works of His own hands. Everything is supposed to be ordered according to impersonal and abstract "laws of Nature." Thus is the Creator banished from His own creation. Therefore we need not be surprised that men, in their degraded conceptions, exclude Him from the realm of human affairs. Throughout Christendom, with an almost negligible exception, the theory is held that man determines his fortunes and decides his destiny by his own "free-will." That Satan is to be blamed for much of the evil which is in the world, is freely affirmed by those who, though having much to say about "the responsibility of man," often *deny* their *own* responsibility, by attributing to the Devil what, in fact, proceeds from their *own* evil hearts (Mark 7: 21-23).

But who *is* regulating affairs on this earth today—God, or the Devil? Attempt to take a serious and comprehensive view of the world. What a scene of confusion and chaos confronts us on every side! Sin is rampant; lawlessness abounds; evil men and seducers *are* waxing "worse and worse" (2 Tim. 3: 13). Today, everything appears to be *out of joint*. Thrones are creaking and tottering, ancient dynasties are being overturned, nations are in revolt, civilization is a demonstrated failure; half of Christendom was but recently locked together in a death grapple; and now that the titanic conflict is over, instead of the world having been made ' safe for democracy," we have discovered that democracy is very *unsafe* for the world. Unrest, discontent, and lawlessness are rife everywhere, and none can say how soon another great war will be set in motion. Statesmen are perplexed and staggered. Men's hearts are " failing them for fear, and for looking after those things which are coming on the earth " (Luke 21: 26). Do *these* things look as though *God* had full control?

But let us confine our attention to the religious realm. After nineteen centuries of Gospel preaching, Christ is still " despised and rejected of men." Worse still, *He* (the Christ of Scripture) is proclaimed and magnified by very few. In the majority of modern pulpits He is dishonoured and disowned. Despite frantic efforts to attract the crowds, the majority of the churches are being emptied rather than filled. And what of the great masses of non-churchgoers? In the light of Scripture we are compelled to believe that the " many " are on the broad road that leadeth to destruction, and that " few " are on the narrow way that leadeth unto life. Many are declaring that Christianity is a failure, and despair is settling on many faces. Not a few of the Lord's own people are bewildered, and their faith is being severely tried. *And what of God?* Does He see and hear? Is He impotent or indifferent? A number of those who are regarded as leaders of Christian thought told us that God could not prevent the coming of the late awful War, and that He was *unable* to bring about its termination. It was said, and said openly, that conditions were *beyond* God's control. Do these things look as though *God* were ruling the world?

Who *is* regulating affairs on this earth today—God, or the Devil? What impression is made upon the minds of those men of the world who, occasionally, attend a Gospel service? What are the conceptions formed by those who hear even those preachers who are counted as " orthodox "? Is it not that a *disappointed* God is the One whom Christians believe in? From what is heard from the average evangelist today, is not any serious hearer *obliged* to conclude that he professes to represent a God who is filled with benevolent intentions, yet unable to carry them out; that He is earnestly desirous of blessing men, but that they will not let Him? Then, *must not* the average hearer draw the inference that the Devil has gained the upper hand, and that God is to be pitied rather than worshipped.

But does not everything seem to show that the Devil *has* far more to do with the affairs of earth than God has? Ah, it all depends upon whether we are walking by faith, or walking by sight. Are your thoughts, my reader, concerning this world and God's relation to it, based upon what you *see*? Face this question seriously and honestly. And if you are a Christian, you will, most probably, have cause to bow your head with shame and sorrow, and to acknowledge that it *is* so. Alas, in reality, we walk very little " by faith." But what does " walking by faith " signify? It means that our thoughts are formed, our actions regulated, our lives moulded by the Holy Scriptures, for, " faith cometh by hearing, and hearing *by the Word of God*" (Rom. 10: 17). It is from the Word of Truth, and that alone, that we can learn what is *God's* relation to this world.

Who is regulating affairs on this earth today—God, or the Devil? *What saith the Scriptures?* Ere we consider the direct reply to this query, let it be said that the Scriptures *predicted* just what we now see and hear. The prophecy of Jude is in course of fulfilment. It would lead us too far astray from our present inquiry fully to amplify this assertion, but what we have particularly in mind is a sentence in verse 8—" Likewise also these filthy dreamers defile the flesh, *despise dominion, and speak evil of dignities*." Yes, they " speak evil " of the Supreme Dignity, the " Only Potentate, the Kings of kings, and Lord of lords." Ours is peculiarly an age of irreverence, and as a consequence, the spirit of lawlessness, which brooks no restraint and which is desirous of casting off everything which interferes with the free course of self-will, is rapidly engulfing the earth like some gigantic tidal wave. The members of the rising generation are the most flagrant offenders, and in the decay and disappearance of parental authority we have the certain precursor of the break up of civic authority. Therefore, in view of the growing disrespect for human law and the refusal to "render honour to whom honour is due," we need not be surprised that the recognition of the majesty, the authority, the sovereignty of the Almighty Law-giver should recede more and more into the background, and that the masses have less and less patience with those who insist upon them.

Who is regulating affairs on this earth today—God, or the Devil? What saith the Scriptures? If we believe their plain and positive declarations, no room is left for uncertainty. They affirm, again and again, that God is on the throne of the universe; that the sceptre is in His hands; that He is directing *all things* "after the counsel of His own will." They affirm, not only that God created all things, but also that God is ruling and reigning over all the works of His hands. They affirm that God is the "Almighty," that His will is irreversible, that He is absolute sovereign in every realm of all His vast dominions. And surely it *must* be so. Only two alternatives are possible: God must either rule, or be ruled; sway, or be swayed; accomplish His own will, or be thwarted by His creatures. Accepting the fact that He is the "Most High," the only Potentate and King of kings, vested with perfect wisdom and illimitable power, the conclusion is irresistible that He must be God *in fact,* as well as in name.

It is in view of what we have briefly referred to above, that we say, Present-day conditions call loudly for a new examination and new presentation of God's omnipotency, God's sufficiency, God's sovereignty. From every pulpit in the land it needs to be thundered forth that God still lives, that God still observes, that God still reigns. Faith is now in the crucible, it is being tested by fire, and there is no fixed and sufficient resting-place for the heart and mind but in *the Throne of God.* What is needed now, as never before, is a full, positive, constructive setting forth of the Godhood of God. Drastic diseases call for drastic remedies. People are weary of platitudes and mere generalizations—the call is for something definite and specific. Soothing-syrup may serve for peevish children, but an iron tonic is better suited for adults, and we know of nothing which is more calculated to infuse spiritual vigour into our frames than a Scriptural apprehension of the full character of God. It is written, " The people that do *know their God* shall be strong and do exploits " (Dan. 11 : 32).

Without a doubt a world-crisis is at hand, and everywhere men are alarmed. But God is not ! *He* is never taken by surprise. It is no unexpected emergency which now confronts Him, for He is the One who " worketh all things after the counsel of His own will " (Eph. 1 : 11). Hence, though the world is panic-stricken, the word to the believer is, " Fear not " ! " All things " are subject to His immediate control : " all things " are moving in accord with His eternal purpose, and therefore, " all things " are " working together *for good* to them that love God, to them who are the called according to His purpose." It *must* be so, for " of Him, and through Him, and to Him are *all things*" (Rom. 11 : 36). Yet how little is this realized today even by the people of God ! Many suppose that He is little more than a far-distant Spectator, taking no immediate hand in the affairs of earth. It is true that man has a will, but so also has God. It is true that man is endowed with power, but God is all-powerful. It is true that, speaking generally, the material world is regulated by law, but behind that law is the law-Giver and law-Administrator. Man is but the creature. God is the Creator, and endless ages before man first saw the light " the mighty God " (Isa. 9 : 6) existed, and ere the world was founded, made His plans; and being infinite in power and man only finite, His purpose and plan cannot be withstood or thwarted by the creatures of His own hands.

We readily acknowledge that life is a profound problem, and that we are surrounded by mystery on every side; but we are not like the beasts of the field—ignorant of their origin, and unconscious of what is before them. No: "*We have* also a more sure Word of Prophecy," of which it is said, "whereunto ye do well that ye take heed, as unto a light that shineth in a dark place, until the day dawn, and the day star arise in your hearts" (2 Pet. 1: 19). And it is to this Word of Prophecy we indeed do well to " take heed," to that Word which had not its origin in the mind of man but in the Mind of God, for " the prophecy came not at any time by the will of man; but holy men of God spake moved by the Holy Spirit." We say again, it is to *this* " *Word* " we do well to take heed. As we turn to this Word and are instructed by it, we discover a fundamental principle which must be applied to every problem: Instead of beginning with man and his world and working back to God, we must begin with God and work down to man—" In the beginning *God* "! Apply this principle to the present situation. Begin with the world as it is today and try to work back to God, and everything will seem to show that God has no connection with the world at all. But begin with God and work down to the world, and light, much light, is cast on the problem. Because God is *holy* His anger burns against sin; because God is *righteous* His judgments fall upon those who rebel against Him; because God is *faithful* the solemn threatenings of His Word are fulfilled; because God is *omnipotent* none can successfully resist Him, still less overthrow His counsel; and because God is *omniscient* no problem can master Him and no difficulty baffle His wisdom. It is just because God is who He is and what He is that we are now beholding on earth what we do—the beginning of His outpoured judgments: in view of His inflexible justice and immaculate holiness we could not expect anything other than what is now spread before our eyes.

But let it be said very emphatically that the heart can only rest upon and *enjoy* the blessed truth of the absolute sovereignty of God as *faith is in exercise*. Faith is ever occupied with *God*. That is the character of it; that is what differentiates it from intellectual theology. Faith *endures* " as seeing Him who is invisible " (Heb. 11:27); endures the disap-

pointments, the hardships, and the heart-aches of life, by re-
cognizing that all comes from the hand of Him who is too
wise to err and too loving to be unkind. But so long as we
are occupied with any other object than God Himself, there
will be neither rest for the heart nor peace for the mind. But
when we receive all that enters our lives as from *His* hand,
then, no matter what may be our circumstances or surround-
ings—whether in a hovel or prison-dungeon, or at a martyr's
stake—we shall be enabled to say, "The lines are fallen unto
me in *pleasant places*" (Ps. 16: 6). But *that* is the language
of *faith*, not of sight nor of sense.

But if instead of bowing to the testimony of Holy Writ,
if instead of walking by faith, we follow the evidence of our
eyes, and *reason* therefrom, we shall fall into a quagmire of
virtual atheism. Or, if we are regulated by the opinions and
views of others, peace will be at an end. Granted that there
is much in this world of sin and suffering which appals and
saddens us; granted that there is much in the providential
dealings of God which startle and stagger us; that is no
reason why we should unite with the unbelieving worldling
who says, "If I were God, I would not allow this or tolerate
that." Better far, in the presense of bewildering mystery,
to say with one of old, "I was dumb, I opened not my
mouth; because Thou didst it" (Ps. 39: 9). Scripture tells
us that God's judgments *are* "unsearchable," and His
ways "past finding out" (Rom. 11: 33). It must be so if
faith is to be tested, confidence in His wisdom and righteousness strengthened, and submission to His holy will fos-
tered.

Here is the fundamental difference between the man of
faith and the man of unbelief. The unbeliever is "of the
world," judges everything by worldly standards, views life
from the standpoint of time and sense, and weighs everything
in the balances of his own carnal understanding. But the
man of faith *brings in God*, looks at everything from *His*
standpoint, estimates values by spiritual standards, and views
life in the light of eternity. Doing this, he receives whatever
comes as from the hand of God. Doing this, his heart is calm

in the midst of the storm.   Doing this, he rejoices in hope of the glory of God.

We are well aware that what we have written is in open opposition to much of the teaching that is current both in religious literature and in the representative pulpits of the land. We freely grant that the postulate of God's Sovereignty with all its corollaries is at direct variance with the opinions and thoughts of the natural man, but the truth is, the natural man is quite *unable* to think upon these matters: he is not competent to form a proper estimate of God's character and ways, and it is because of this that God has given us a revelation of *His* mind, and in that revelation He plainly declares, " My thoughts are not your thoughts, neither are your ways My ways, saith the Lord. For as the heavens are higher than the earth, so are My ways higher than your ways, and My thoughts than your thoughts " (Isa. 55 : 8, 9).   In view of this scripture, it is only to be expected that much of the contents of the Bible *conflicts* with the sentiments of the carnal mind, which is *enmity* against God.   Our appeal then is not to the popular beliefs of the day, nor to the creeds of the churches, but to the Law and Testimony of Jehovah. All that we ask for is an impartial and attentive examination of what we have written, and that, made prayerfully in the light of the Lamp of Truth.   May the reader heed the Divine admonition to " prove all things; hold fast that which is good " (1 Thess. 5 : 21).

THE SOVEREIGNTY OF GOD DEFINED

"Thine, O Lord, is the greatness, and the power, and the
glory, and the victory, and the majesty: for all that is
in the heaven and in the earth is Thine; Thine is the
kingdom, O Lord, *and Thou art exalted as Head above
all*" (1 CHRON. 29:11).

THE "Sovereignty of God" is an expression that once
was generally understood. It was a phrase commonly
used in religious literature. It was a theme frequently expounded in the pulpit. It was a truth which brought comfort to many hearts, and gave virility and stability to Christian
character. But, today, to make mention of God's sovereignty
is, in many quarters, to speak in an unknown tongue. Were
we to announce from the average pulpit that the subject of
our discourse would be the sovereignty of God, it would
sound very much as though we had borrowed a phrase from
one of the dead languages. Alas! that it should be so. Alas!
that the doctrine which is the key to history, the interpreter
of Providence, the warp and woof of Scripture, and the
foundation of Christian theology, should be so sadly neglected and so little understood.

The sovereignty of God! What do we mean by this expression? We mean the supremacy of God, the kingship of
God, the Godhood of God. To say that God is sovereign is
to declare that God *is* God. To say that God is sovereign is
to declare that He is the Most High, doing according to His
will in the army of heaven, and among the inhabitants of the
earth, so that none can stay His hand or say unto Him, What
doest Thou? (Dan. 4:35). To say that God is sovereign is
to declare that He is the Almighty, the Possessor of all power
in heaven and earth, so that none can defeat His counsels,
thwart His purposes, or resist His will (Ps. 115:3). To say
that God is sovereign is to declare that He is "The Governor

20

among the nations " (Ps. 22 : 28), setting up kingdoms, over throwing empires, and determining the course of dynasties as pleaseth Him best. To say that God is sovereign is to declare that He is the " Only Potentate, the King of kings, and Lord of lords " (1 Tim. 6 : 15). Such is the God of the Bible.

How different is the God of the Bible from the God of modern Christendom! The conception of Deity which prevails most widely today, even among those who profess to give heed to the Scriptures, is a miserable caricature, a pathetic travesty of the Truth. The God of the twentieth century is a helpless, effeminate being who commands the respect of no really thoughtful man. The God of the popular mind is the creation of a maudlin sentimentality. The God of many a present-day pulpit is an object of pity rather than of awe-inspiring reverence.[1] To say that God the Father has purposed the salvation of all mankind, that God the Son died with the express intention of saving the whole human race, and that God the Holy Spirit is now seeking to win the world to Christ; when, as a matter of common observation, it is apparent that the great majority of our fellow-men are dying in sin, and passing into a hopeless eternity: is to say that God the Father is *disappointed*, that God the Son is *dissatisfied*, and that God the Holy Spirit is *defeated*. We have stated the issue baldly, but there is no escaping the conclusion. To argue that God is " trying His best " to save all mankind, but that the majority of men will not let Him save them, is to imply that the will of the Creator is impotent, and that the will of the creature is omnipotent. To throw the blame, as many do, upon the Devil, does not remove the difficulty, for if Satan is defeating the purpose of God, then Satan is Almighty and God is no longer the Supreme Being.

To declare that the Creator's original plan has been frustrated by sin, is to *dethrone* God. To suggest that God was taken by surprise in Eden and that He is now attempting to

---

[1] Some years ago an "evangelical" preacher of nation-wide reputation visited the town in which we then were, and during the course of his address kept repeating "Poor God! Poor God!" Surely it is this preacher who needs to be pitied!

remedy an unforeseen calamity, is to *degrade* the Most High to the level of a finite, erring mortal. To argue that man is the sole determiner of his own destiny, and that therefore he has the power to checkmate his Maker, is to *strip* God of the attribute of Omnipotence. To say that the creature has burst the bounds assigned by his Creator, and that God is now practically a helpless Spectator of the sin and suffering entailed by Adam's fall, is to *repudiate* the express declaration of Holy Writ, namely, "Surely the wrath of man shall praise Thee: the remainder of wrath *shalt Thou restrain*" (Ps. 76: 10). In a word, to deny the sovereignty of God is to enter upon a path which, if followed to its logical terminus, leads to blank atheism.

The sovereignty of the God of Scripture is absolute, irresistible, infinite. When we say that God is sovereign, we affirm His right to govern the universe, which He has made for His own glory, just as He pleases. We affirm that *His right* is the right of the Potter over the clay, viz: that He may mould that clay into whatsoever form He chooses, fashioning out of *the same lump* one vessel unto honour and another unto dishonour. We affirm that He is under no rule or law outside His own will and nature, *that God is a law unto Himself*, and that He is under no obligation to give an account of His matters to any.

Sovereignty characterizes the whole Being of God. He is sovereign in all His attributes. *He is sovereign in the exercise of His power*. His power is exercised *as* He wills, *when* He wills, *where* He wills. This fact is evidenced on every page of Scripture. For a long season that power appears to be dormant, and then it goes forth with irresistible might. Pharaoh dared to hinder Israel from going forth to worship Jehovah in the wilderness. What happened? God exercised His power, His people were delivered and their cruel taskmasters slain. But a little later, the Amalekites dared to attack these same Israelites in the wilderness, and what happened? Did God put forth His power on this occasion and display His hand as He did at the Red Sea? Were these enemies of His people promptly overthrown and destroyed?

No, on the contrary, the Lord swore that He would " have war with Amalek from *generation to generation*" (Ex. 17:16). Again, when Israel entered the land of Canaan, God's power was signally displayed. The city of Jericho barred their progress. What happened? Israel did not draw a bow nor strike a blow: the Lord stretched forth His hand and the walls fell down flat. But the miracle was never repeated! *No other city fell after this manner*. Every other city had to be captured by the sword!

Many other instances might be adduced illustrating the sovereign exercise of God's power. God put forth His power and David was delivered from Goliath the giant; the mouths of the lions were closed and Daniel escaped unhurt; the three Hebrew children were cast into the burning fiery furnace and came forth unharmed and unscorched. *But God's power did not always interpose for the deliverance of His people*, for we read: "*And others* had trial of cruel mockings and scourgings, yea, moreover of bonds and imprisonment: they were stoned, they were sawn asunder, were tempted, were slain with the sword; they wandered about in sheepskins and goatskins; being destitute, afflicted, tormented " (Heb. 11: 36, 37). But why? Why were not these men of faith delivered like the others? Or, why were not the others suffered to be killed as were these? Why should God's power interpose and rescue some and not others? Why did He allow Stephen to be stoned to death, and then deliver Peter from prison?

God is sovereign in the *delegation of His power to others*. Why did God endow Methuselah with a vitality which enabled him to outlive all his contemporaries? Why did God impart to Samson a physical strength which no other human has ever possessed? Again, it is written, " But thou shalt remember the Lord thy God: for it is He that *giveth thee power* to get wealth " (Deut. 8: 18), but God does not bestow this power on all alike. Why not? Why has He given such power to men like Carnegie and Rockefeller? The answer to all of these questions is, Because God is Sovereign, and being Sovereign He does as He pleases.

God is sovereign in the exercise of His mercy. Necessarily so, for mercy is directed by the *will* of Him that showeth mercy. Mercy is not a *right* to which man is entitled. Mercy is that adorable attribute of God by which He pities and relieves the wretched. But under the righteous government of God no one is wretched who does not *deserve* to be so. The objects of mercy, then, are those who are miserable, and misery is the result of *sin*; hence the miserable are deserving of punishment, not mercy. To speak of *deserving mercy* is a contradiction of terms.

The sovereign exercise of God's mercy—pity shown to the wretched—was displayed when Jehovah became flesh and tabernacled among men. Take one illustration. During one of the Feasts of the Jews, the Lord Jesus went up to Jerusalem. He came to the Pool of Bethesda, where lay "*a great multitude* of impotent folk, of blind, halt, withered, waiting for the moving of the water." Among this "great multitude" there was "a certain man which had an infirmity thirty and eight years." What happened? "When Jesus saw *him* lie, and knew that he had been now a long time in that case, he saith *unto him,* Wilt thou be made whole? The impotent man answered Him, Sir, I have no man, when the water is troubled, to put me into the pool: but while I am coming, another steppeth down before me. Jesus saith unto him, Rise, take up thy bed, and walk. And immediately the man was made whole, and took up his bed, and walked" (John 5: 1-9). Why was this one man singled out from all the others? We are not told that he cried "Lord, have mercy *on me.*" There is not a word in the narrative which intimates that this man possessed any qualifications which entitled him to receive special favour. Here then was a case of the sovereign exercise of Divine mercy, for it was just as easy for Christ to heal the whole of that "great multitude" as this one "certain man." But He did not. He put forth His power and relieved the wretchedness of this one particular sufferer, and for some reason known only to Himself, He refrained from doing the same for the others.

God is sovereign in the exercise of His grace: necessarily so, for grace is favour shown to the *undeserving,* yea, to the

Hell-deserving. Grace is the antithesis of justice. Justice demands the impartial enforcement of law. Justice requires that each shall receive his legitimate due, neither more nor less. Justice bestows no favours and is no respecter of persons. Justice, as such, shows no pity and knows no mercy. Divine grace is not exercised at the expense of justice, but "grace reigns through righteousness" (Rom. 5:21), and if grace "*reigns*," then is grace sovereign.

Grace has been defined as the unmerited favour of God;[1] and if unmerited, then none can claim it as their inalienable *right*. If grace is unearned and undeserved, then none are *entitled* to it. If grace is a gift, then none can *demand* it. Therefore, as salvation is by grace, the free gift of God, then He bestows it on whom He pleases. Because salvation is by grace, the very chief of sinners is not beyond the reach of Divine mercy. Because salvation is by grace, boasting is excluded and God gets all the glory.

The sovereign exercise of grace is illustrated on nearly every page of Scripture. The Gentiles are left to walk in their own ways, while Israel becomes the covenant people of Jehovah. Ishmael the firstborn is cast out comparatively unblest, while Isaac, the son of his parents' old age, is made the child of promise. Esau the generous-hearted is denied the blessing, while the worm Jacob receives the inheritance and is fashioned into a vessel of honour. So in the New Testament. Divine truth is hidden from the wise and prudent, but is revealed to babes. The Pharisees and Sadducees are left to go their own way, while publicans and harlots are drawn by the cords of love.

In a remarkable manner Divine grace was exercised at the time of the Saviour's birth. The incarnation of God's Son was one of the greatest events in the history of the universe,

[1] An esteemed friend who kindly read through this book in its manuscript form, and to whom we are indebted for a number of excellent suggestions, has pointed out that grace is something more than "unmerited favour." To feed a tramp who calls on me is "unmerited favour," but it is scarcely *grace*. But suppose that after he has robbed me I should feed this starving tramp—*that* would be "grace." Grace, then, is favour shown where there is positive *demerit* in the one receiving it.

and yet its actual occurrence was not made known to all mankind; instead, it was specially revealed to the Bethlehem shepherds and wise men of the East. And this was prophetic and indicative of the entire course of this dispensation, for even today Christ is not made known to all. It would have been an easy matter for God to have sent a company of angels to *every nation* and announced the birth of His Son. But He did not. God could have readily attracted the attention of all mankind to the " star "; but He did not. Why? Because God is sovereign and dispenses His favours as He pleases. Note particularly the two classes to whom the birth of the Saviour *was* made known, namely, the most *unlikely* classes—shepherds and Gentiles from a far country. No angel stood before the Sanhedrin and announced the advent of Israel's Messiah! No " star " appeared unto the scribes and lawyers as they, in their pride and self-righteousness, searched the Scriptures! They searched diligently to find out where He should be born, and yet it was not made known *to them* He was actually come. What a display of Divine sovereignty —humble shepherds singled out for peculiar honour, and the learned and eminent passed by! And why was the birth of the Saviour revealed to these foreigners, and not to those in whose midst He was born? See in this a wonderful fore-shadowing of God's dealings with our race throughout the entire Christian dispensation—sovereign in the exercise of His grace, bestowing His favours on whom He pleases, often on the most unlikely and unworthy.

THE SOVEREIGNTY OF GOD IN CREATION

" Thou art worthy, O Lord, to receive glory, and honour, and power: for Thou has created all things, and for Thy pleasure they are and were created " (REV. 4 : 11).

HAVING seen that sovereignty characterizes the whole Being of God, let us now observe how it marks all His ways and dealings.

In the great expanse of eternity, which stretches behind Genesis 1 : 1, the universe was unborn and creation existed only in the mind of the great Creator. In His sovereign majesty God dwelt alone. We refer to that far distant period before the heavens and the earth were created. But even at that time, if time it could be called, God was sovereign. He might create or not create *according to His own good pleasure*. He might create this way or that way; He might create one world or one million worlds, and who was there to resist His will? He might call into existence a million different creatures and place them on *absolute equality*, endowing them with the same faculties and placing them in the same environment; or, He might create a million creatures each *differing* from the others, and possessing nothing in common save their creaturehood; and who was there to challenge His right? If He so pleased, He might call into existence a world so immense that its dimensions were utterly beyond finite computation; and were He so disposed, He might create an organism so small that not even the most powerful microscope could reveal its existence to human eyes. It was His sovereign right to create, on the one hand, the exalted seraphim to burn around His throne, and on the other hand, the tiny insect which dies the same hour that it is born. If the mighty God chose to have *one vast gradation* in His universe, from loftiest seraph to creeping reptile, from revolving worlds to floating atoms, from macrocosm to microcosm, *instead of complete uniformity*, who was there to question His sovereign pleasure?

Behold then the exercise of Divine sovereignty long before man ever saw the light. With whom took God counsel in the creation and disposition of His creatures? See the birds as they fly through the air, the beasts as they roam the earth, the fishes as they swim in the sea, and then ask, Who was it that made them to differ? Was it not their Creator who *sovereignly* assigned their various locations and adaptations to them!

Turn your eye to the heavens and observe the mysteries of Divine sovereignty which there confront the thoughtful beholder: "There is one glory of the sun, and another glory of the moon, and another glory of the stars: for one star *differeth from* another star in glory" (1 Cor. 15: 41). But why should they? Why should the sun be more glorious than the circling planets? Why should there be stars of the first magnitude and others of the tenth? Why such amazing *inequalities*? And why should there be "shooting stars," "falling stars, "wandering star" (Jude 13), in a word, *ruined* stars? And the only possible answer is, "For Thy pleasure they are and were created" (Rev. 4: 11).

Come now to our own planet. Why should two thirds of its surface be covered with water, and why should so much of its remaining third be unfit for human cultivation or habitation? Why should there be vast stretches of marshes, deserts and ice-fields? Why should one country be so inferior, topographically, to another? Why should one be fertile, and another almost barren? Why should one be rich in minerals and another produce none? Why should the climate of one be congenial and healthy, and another the reverse? Why should one abound in rivers and lakes, and another be almost devoid of them? Why should one be constantly troubled with earthquakes, and another almost entirely free from them? Why? Because thus it pleased the Creator and Upholder of all things.

Look at the animal kingdom and note the wondrous

variety. What comparison is possible between the lion and the lamb, the bear and the kid, the elephant and the mouse? Some, like the horse and the dog, are gifted with great intelligence; while others, like sheep and swine, are almost devoid of it. Why? Some are designed to be beasts of burden, while others enjoy a life of freedom. But why should the mule and the donkey be shackled to a life of drudgery, while the lion and tiger are allowed to roam the jungle at their pleasure? Some are fit for food, others unfit; some are beautiful, others ugly; some are endowed with great strength, others seem quite helpless; some are fleet of foot, others can scarcely crawl—contrast the hare and the tortoise; some are of use to man, others appear to be quite valueless; some live for years, others a few months at most; some are tame, others fierce. But why all these variations and differences?

What is true of the animals is equally true of the birds and fishes. But consider now the *vegetable kingdom*. Why should roses have thorns, and lilies grow without them? Why should one flower emit a fragrant aroma and another have none? Why should one tree bear fruit which is wholesome and another that which is poisonous? Why should one vegetable be capable of enduring frost and another wither under it? Why should one apple tree be loaded with fruit, and another tree of the same age and in the same orchard be almost barren? Why should one plant flower a dozen times in a year and another bear blossoms but once a century? Truly, "*whatsoever the Lord pleased*, that did He in heaven, and in earth, in the seas, and all deep places" (Ps. 135: 6).

Consider the angelic hosts. Surely we shall find uniformity here. But no; there, as elsewhere, the same sovereign pleasure of the Creator is displayed. Some are higher in rank than others; some are more powerful than others; some are nearer to God than others. Scripture reveals a definite and well-defined gradation in the angelic orders. From archangel, past seraphim and cherubim, we come to "principalities and powers" (Eph. 3: 10), and from principalities and powers to "rulers" (Eph. 6: 12), and then to the angels them-

selves, and even among them we read of " the *elect* angels "
(1 Tim. 5: 21). Again we ask, Why this *inequality*, this difference in rank and order? And all we can say is " Our God
is in the heavens; He hath done whatsoever He hath pleased "
(Ps. 115: 3).

If then we see the sovereignty of God displayed throughout all creation why should it be thought a strange thing if
we behold it operating in the midst of the *human family*?
Why should it be thought strange if to one God is pleased to
give five talents and to another only one? Why should it be
thought strange if one is born with a robust constitution and
another, having the same parents, is frail and sickly? Why
should it be thought strange if Abel is cut off in his prime,
while Cain is suffered to live on for years? Why should it be
thought strange that some should be born black and others
white; some be born idiots and others with high intellectual
endowments; some be born constitutionally lethargic and
others full of energy; some be born with a temperament that
is selfish, fiery, egotistical, others who are naturally self-sacri-
ficing, submissive and meek? Why should it be thought
strange if some are qualified by nature to lead and rule, while
others are only fitted to follow and serve? Heredity and environment cannot account for all these variations and inequalities. No; it is *God* who maketh one to differ from
another. Why should He? " Even so, Father: for so it
seemed good in Thy sight " (Matt. 11: 26) must be our reply.

Learn then this basic truth, that the Creator is absolute
Sovereign, executing His own will, performing His own pleasure, and considering nought but His own glory. " *The Lord
hath made all things FOR HIMSELF* " (Prov. 16: 4). And
had He not a perfect *right* to do so? Since God *is* God, who
dare challenge His prerogative? To murmur against Him
is rank rebellion. To question His ways is to impugn His
wisdom. To criticize Him is sin of the deepest dye. Have
we forgotten *who* He is? Behold, " All nations before Him
are as nothing; and they are counted to Him less than nothing, and vanity. To whom then will ye liken God?" (Isaiah
40: 17, 18).

THE SOVEREIGNTY OF GOD IN ADMINISTRATION

"The Lord hath prepared His Throne in the heavens; *and His Kingdom ruleth over all*" (Ps. 103:19).

FIRST, a word concerning the *need* for God to govern *the material world*. Suppose the opposite for a moment. For the sake of argument, let us suppose that God created the world, designed and fixed certain laws (which men term "the laws of Nature"), and that He then *withdrew*, leaving the world to its fortune and the out-working of these laws. In such a case, we should have a world over which there was no intelligent, presiding Governor, a world controlled by nothing more than *impersonal* laws—a concept worthy of gross Materialism and blank Atheism. But, I say, suppose it for a moment; and in the light of such a supposition, weigh well the following question: What guarantee have we that some day ere long the world will not be destroyed? "The wind bloweth *where it listeth*" (pleaseth), which means that man can neither harness nor hinder it. Sometimes the wind blows with great fury, and it might be that it should suddenly gather in volume and velocity, until it became a hurricane earth-wide in its range. If there is nothing more than the laws of Nature regulating the wind, then, perhaps to-morrow, there may come a terrific tornado and sweep everything on the surface of the earth to destruction. What assurance have we against such a calamity? Again; of late years we have heard and read much about clouds bursting and flooding whole districts, working fearful havoc in the destruction of both property and life. Man is helpless before them, for science can devise no means to *prevent* clouds bursting. Then how do we know that these bursting-clouds will not be multiplied indefinitely and the whole earth be deluged by their downpour? This would be nothing new:

31

why should not the Flood of Noah's day be repeated? And what of earthquakes? Every few years, some island or some great city is swept out of existence by one of them—and what can man do? Where is the guarantee that ere long a mammoth earthquake will not destroy the whole world? Surely every reader now sees the point we are seeking to make: Deny that God is *governing* matter, deny that *He* is "upholding all things by the word of His power" (Heb. 1:3), *and all sense of security is gone!*

Let us pursue a similar course of reasoning in connection with the *human race.* Is God governing this world of ours? Is He shaping the destinies of nations, controlling the course of empires, determining the limits of dynasties? Has He prescribed the limits of evil-doers, saying, Thus far shalt thou go and no farther? Let us suppose the opposite for a moment. Let us assume that God has delivered over the helm into the hand of His creatures, and see where such a supposition leads us. For the sake of argument we will suppose that every man enters this world endowed with a will that is absolutely free, and that it is *impossible* to control him without *destroying* his freedom. If this were so, we have no guarantee against the entire human race committing moral suicide. Let all Divine restraints be removed and man be left absolutely free to do as *he* pleases, then all ethical distinctions would soon disappear, the spirit of barbarism would prevail universally, and pandemonium would reign supreme. Why not? If one nation deposes its rulers and repudiates its constitution, what is there to prevent all nations from doing the same? If little more than a century ago the streets of Paris ran with the blood of rioters, what assurance have we that before the present century closes every city throughout the world will not witness a similar sight? What is there to hinder earthwide lawlessness and universal anarchy? Thus we have sought to show the *need*, the imperative need, for God to occupy the Throne, take the government upon *His* shoulder, and control the activities and destinies of His creatures.

Having shown, in brief, the imperative need for God to

reign over our world, let us now observe further the *fact* that God *does* rule, actually rule, and that His government extends to and is exercised over all things and all creatures.

1. GOD GOVERNS INANIMATE MATTER.

That God governs inanimate matter, that inanimate matter performs His bidding and fulfils His decrees, is clearly shown on the very frontispiece of Divine revelation. God said, "Let there be light," and "*There was light.*" God said, "Let the waters under the heaven be gathered together unto one place, and let the dry land appear: and *it was so.*" And again, "God said, Let the earth bring forth grass, the herb yielding seed, and the fruit tree yielding fruit after his kind, whose seed is in itself, upon the earth: *and it was so.*" As the Psalmist declares, "He spake, and it was done; He commanded, and it stood fast."

What is stated in the first chapter of Genesis is afterwards illustrated all through the Bible. When the iniquities of the antediluvians had come to the full, then God said, "And, behold, *I, even I, do bring a flood of waters upon the earth*, to destroy all flesh, wherein is the breath of life, from under heaven; and everything that is in the earth shall die"; and in fulfilment of this we read, "In the six hundredth year of Noah's life, in the second month, the seventeenth day of the month, the same day were all the fountains of the great deep broken up, and the windows of heaven were opened. And the rain was upon the earth forty days and forty nights" (Gen. 6: 17 and 7: 11, 12).

Witness God's absolute (and *sovereign*) control of inanimate matter in connection with the plagues upon Egypt. At His bidding the light was turned into darkness and a river into blood; hail fell, and death came down upon the godless land of the Nile, until even its haughty monarch was compelled to cry out for deliverance. Note particularly how the inspired record here emphasizes God's absolute control over the elements—"And Moses stretched forth his rod toward heaven: *and the Lord sent* thunder and hail, and the fire ran along upon the ground; *and the Lord* rained hail upon the land of Egypt. So there was hail, and fire mingled with the hail, very grievous, such as there was none like it in all the land of Egypt since it became a nation. And the hail smote throughout all the land of Egypt all that was in the field, both man and beast; and the hail smote every herb of the field, and brake every tree of the field. *Only in the land of Goshen, where the children of Israel were, was there no hail* " (Ex. 9: 23-26). The same distinction was observed in connection with the ninth plague: " And the Lord said unto Moses, Stretch out thine hand toward heaven, that there may be darkness over the land of Egypt, even darkness which may be felt. And Moses stretched forth his hand toward heaven; and there was a thick darkness in all the land of Egypt three days: They saw not one another, neither rose any from his place for three days: *but all the children of Israel had light in their dwellings* " (Ex. 10: 21-23).

The above examples are by no means *isolated* cases. At God's decree fire and brimstone descended from heaven and the cities of the Plain were destroyed, and a fertile valley was converted into a loathsome sea of death. At His bidding the waters of the Red Sea parted asunder so that the Israelites passed over dry shod, and at His word they rolled back again and destroyed the Egyptians who were pursuing them. A word from Him, and the earth opened her mouth and Korah and his rebellious company were swallowed up. The furnace of Nebuchadnezzar was heated " one seven times " beyond its normal temperature, and into it three of God's children were cast, but the fire did not so much as scorch their clothes, though it slew the men who cast them into it.

What a demonstration of the Creator's governmental control over the elements was furnished when He became flesh and tabernacled among men! Behold Him asleep in the boat. A storm arises. The winds roar and the waves are lashed into fury. The disciples who are with Him, fearful lest their little craft should founder, awake their Master, saying, " Carest Thou not that we perish?" And then we read, " And He arose, and rebuked the wind, and said unto the sea, Peace, be still. *And the wind ceased, and there was a great calm*" (Mark 4: 39). Mark again, the sea, at the will of its Creator, bore Him up upon its waves. At a word from him the fig-tree withered; at His touch disease fled instantly.

The heavenly bodies are also ruled by their Maker and perform His sovereign pleasure. Take two illustrations. At God's bidding the sun went back ten degrees on the dial of Ahaz to help the weak faith of Hezekiah. In New Testament times, God caused a star to herald the incarnation of His Son —the star which appeared unto the wise men of the East. This star, we are told, "*went before them* till it came and stood over where the young Child was" (Matt. 2: 9).

What a declaration is this—" He sendeth forth His commandment upon earth: His word runneth very swiftly. *He giveth* snow like wool: *He scattereth* the hoar frost like ashes. *He casteth forth* His ice like morsels: who can stand before *His cold*? He sendeth out His word, and melteth them: *He causeth His wind to blow*, and the waters flow" (Ps. 147: 15-18). The mutations of the elements are subject to God's sovereign control. It is *God* who withholds the rain, and it is *God* who gives the rain when He wills, where He wills, as He wills, and on whom He wills. Weather Bureaux may attempt to give forecasts of the weather, but how frequently God mocks their calculations! Sun "spots," the varying activities of the planets, the appearing and disappearing of comets (to which abnormal weather is sometimes attributed), atmospheric disturbances, are merely secondary causes, for behind them all is God Himself. Let His Word speak once more: " And also *I have withholden the rain* from you, when there were yet three months to the harvest: *and I caused it* to rain upon one city, and caused it not to rain upon another city: one piece was rained upon, and the piece whereon it rained not withered. So two or three cities wandered unto one city, to drink water; but they were not satisfied: yet have ye not returned unto Me, saith the Lord. *I have smitten you with blasting and mildew*: when your gardens and your vineyards and your fig trees and your olive trees increased, the palmerworm devoured them:

yet have ye not returned unto Me, saith the Lord. *I have sent among you the pestilence* after the manner of Egypt: your young men have I slain with the sword, and have taken away your horses; and I have made the stink of your camps to come up into your nostrils: yet have ye not returned unto Me, saith the Lord" (Amos 4: 7-10).

Truly, then, God governs inanimate matter. Earth and air, fire and water, hail and snow, stormy winds and angry seas, all perform the word of His power and fulfil His sovereign pleasure. Therefore, when we complain about the weather, we are, in reality, murmuring against God.

2. GOD GOVERNS IRRATIONAL CREATURES.

What a striking illustration of God's government over the animal kingdom is found in Gen. 2: 19! "And out of the ground the Lord God formed every beast of the field, and every fowl of the air: *and brought them unto Adam* to see what he would call them: and whatsoever Adam called every living creature, that was the name thereof." Should it be said that this occurred in Eden, and took place before the fall of Adam and the consequent curse which was inflicted on every creature, then our next reference fully meets the objection: God's control of the beasts was again openly displayed at the Flood. Mark how God caused to "come unto" Noah every kind of living creature; "of every living thing of all flesh, two of every sort shalt thou bring into the ark, to keep them alive with thee; they shall be male and female. Of fowls after their kind . . . of every creeping thing of the earth after his kind: two of every sort *shall come unto thee*" (Gen. 6: 19, 20)—all were beneath God's sovereign control. The lion of the jungle, the elephant of the forest, the bear of the polar regions; the ferocious panther, the untamable wolf, the fierce tiger; the high-soaring eagle, and the crawling crocodile—see them all in their native fierceness, and yet quietly submitting to the will of their Creator, and coming two by two into the ark!

We referred to the plagues sent upon Egypt as illustrating God's control of inanimate matter; let us now turn to them again to see how they demonstrate His perfect ruler-ship over irrational creatures. At His word the river brought forth frogs abundantly, and these frogs entered the palace of Pharaoh and the houses of his servants and, contrary to their natural instincts, they entered the beds, the ovens and the kneadingtroughs (Ex. 8: 13). Swarms of flies invaded the land of Egypt, but there were no flies in the land of Goshen! (Ex. 8: 22). Next, the cattle were stricken, and we read, " Behold, *the hand of the Lord* is upon thy cattle which is in the field, upon the horses, upon the asses, upon the camels, upon the oxen, and upon the sheep: there shall be a very grievous murrain. And the Lord shall sever between the cattle of Israel and the cattle of Egypt: and there shall noth-ing die of all that is the children's of Israel. And the Lord appointed a set time, saying, Tomorrow the Lord shall do this thing in the land. And the Lord did that thing on the morrow, and all the cattle of Egypt died: but of the cattle of the children of Israel *died not one*" (Ex. 9: 3-6). In like manner God sent clouds of locusts to plague Pharaoh and his land, appointing the time of their visitation, determining the course and assigning the limits of their depreda-tions.

Angels are not the only ones who do God's bidding. The brute beasts also perform His pleasure. The sacred ark, the ark of the covenant, is in the country of the Philistines. How is it to be brought back to its home-land? Mark the servants of God's choice, and how completely they were be-neath His control: "And the Philistines called for the priests and the diviners saying, What shall we do to the ark of the Lord? tell us wherewith we shall send it to his place. And they said. . . . Now therefore make a new cart, and take two milch kine, on which there hath come no yoke, and tie the kine to the cart, and bring their calves home from them: And take the ark of the Lord, and lay it upon the cart; and put the jewels of gold, which ye return Him for a trespass offering, in a coffer by the side thereof, and send it away that it may go. And see, if it goeth up by the way of his own coast to Beth-shemesh, then He hath done us this great evil:

but if not, then we shall know that it is not His hand that smote us; it was a chance that happened to us." And what happened? How striking the sequel! "And the kine *took the straight way to the way of Beth-shemesh*, and went along the highway, lowing as they went, *and turned not aside to the right hand or to the left*" (1 Sam. 6). Equally striking is the case of Elijah: "And the word of the Lord came unto him, saying, Get thee hence, and hide thyself by the brook Cherith, that is before Jordan. And it shall be, that thou shalt drink of the brook; *and I have commanded the ravens to feed thee there*" (1 Kings 17: 2-4). The natural instinct of these birds of prey was held in subjection, and instead of consuming the food themselves, they carried it to Jehovah's servant in his solitary retreat.

Is further proof required? then it is ready to hand. God makes a dumb ass to rebuke the prophet's madness. He sends forth two she-bears from the woods to devour forty and two of Elisha's tormentors. In fulfilment of His word, He causes the dogs to eat up the flesh of the wicked Jezebel. He seals the mouths of Babylon's lions when Daniel is cast into the den, though, later, He causes them to devour the prophet's accusers. He prepares a great fish to swallow the disobedient Jonah and then, when His ordained hour struck, compelled it to vomit him forth *on dry land*. At His bidding a fish carries a coin to Peter for tribute money in order to fulfil His word. Thus we see that God reigns over irrational creatures: beasts of the field, birds of the air, fishes of the sea, all perform His sovereign *bidding*.

3. GOD GOVERNS THE CHILDREN OF MEN.

We fully appreciate the fact that this is the most difficult part of our subject, and, accordingly, it will be dealt with at greater length in the pages that follow; but at present we consider the *fact* of God's government over men in general, before we attempt to deal with the problem in detail.

Alternatives confront us, and between them we are obliged to choose: either God governs, or He is governed; either

God rules, or He is ruled; either God has His way, or men have theirs. And is our choice between these alternatives hard to make? Shall we say that in man we behold a creature so unruly that he is *beyond* God's control? Shall we say that sin has *alienated* the sinner so far from the thrice Holy One that he is *outside* the pale of His jurisdiction? Or, shall we say that because man has been endowed with moral responsibility God must leave him entirely uncontrolled, at least during the period of his probation? Does it necessarily follow because the natural man is an outlaw against heaven, a rebel against the Divine government, that God is unable to fulfil His purpose through him? We mean, not merely that He may *overrule* the effects of the actions of evil-doers, nor that He will yet bring the wicked to stand before His judgment-bar so that sentence of punishment may be passed upon them—multitudes of non-Christians believe these things—but we mean that every action of the most lawless of His subjects is entirely beneath His control, yea that the actor is, though unknown to himself, carrying out the secret decrees of the Most High. Was it not thus with Judas? and is it possible to select a more extreme case? If, then, the arch-rebel was performing the counsel of God, is it any greater tax upon our faith to believe the same of all rebels?

Our present object is not philosophic inquiry nor metaphysical casuistry, but to ascertain the teaching of Scripture upon this profound theme. To the Law and the Testimony, for there only can we learn of the Divine government—its character, its design, its modus operandi, its scope. What then has it pleased God to reveal to us in His blessed Word concerning His rule over the works of His hands, and particularly, over the one who originally was made in His own image and likeness?

"In Him we live, *and move,* and have our being" (Acts 17: 28). What a sweeping assertion is this! These words, be it noted, were addressed, not to one of the churches of God, not to a company of saints who had reached an exalted plane of spirituality, but to a heathen audience, to those who worshipped " the unknown God " and who "mocked" when they heard of the resurrection of the dead. And yet, to the Athenian philosophers, to the Epicureans and Stoics, the apostle Paul did not hesitate to affirm that they lived and moved and had their being in God, which signified not only that they owed their existence and preservation to the One who made the world and all things therein, but also that their very actions were encompassed and therefore controlled by the Lord of heaven and earth. (Compare Dan. 5: 23, last clause!)

" The *disposings* (margin) of the heart in man, and the answer of the tongue is from the Lord " (Prov. 16: 1). Mark that this declaration is of general application—it is of " man," not simply of believers, that this is predicated. " A man's heart deviseth his way: *but the Lord directeth his steps*" (Prov. 16: 9). If the Lord *directs* the steps of a man, is it not proof that he is being controlled or governed by God? Again: " There are many devices in a man's heart; *nevertheless the counsel of the Lord, that shall stand*" (Prov. 19: 21). Can this mean anything less than that no matter what man may desire and plan, it is the will of his Maker which is executed? As an illustration take the " Rich Fool." The " devices " of his heart are made known to us—" And he thought within himself, saying, What shall I do, because I have no room where to bestow my fruits? And he said, This will I do: *I will* pull down my barns, and build greater; and there *will* I bestow all my fruits and my goods. And I *will* say to my soul, Soul, thou hast much goods laid up for many years; take thine ease, eat, drink, and be merry." Such were the " devices " of his heart, nevertheless it was " the counsel of the Lord " that stood. The " I will's " of the rich man came to nought, for " *God said unto him,* Thou fool, this night thy soul shall be required of thee " (Luke 12: 16-21).

"The king's heart is in the hand of the Lord, as the rivers of water: *He turneth it whithersoever He will*" (Prov. 21: 1). What could be more explicit? Out of the heart are " the issues of life " (Prov. 4: 23), for as a man " thinketh *in his heart*, so is he " (Prov. 23: 7). If then the heart is in the hand of the Lord, and if " He turneth it whithersoever He will," is it not clear that men, yea, governors and rulers, and so *all men*, are completely beneath the governmental control of the Almighty!

No limitations must be placed upon the above declarations. To insist that *some* men, at least, *do* thwart God's will and overturn His counsels, is to repudiate other scriptures equally explicit. Weigh well the following: " But He is in one mind, and who can turn Him? and what His soul desireth, *even that He doeth* " (Job 23: 13). " The counsel of the Lord *standeth for ever*, the thoughts of His heart to all generations " (Ps. 33: 11). " There is no wisdom nor understanding nor counsel against the Lord " (Prov. 21: 30). " For the Lord of hosts hath purposed, *and who shall disannul it*? And His hand is stretched out, and who shall turn it back?" (Isa. 14: 27). " Remember the former things of old: for I am God, and there is none else; I am God, and there is none like Me, declaring the end from the beginning, and from ancient times the things that are not yet done, saying, *My counsel shall stand, and I will do all My pleasure* " (Isa. 46: 9, 10). There is no ambiguity in these passages. They affirm in the most unequivocal and unqualified terms that it is impossible to bring to naught the purpose of Jehovah.

We read the Scriptures in vain if we fail to discover that the actions of men, evil men as well as good, are governed by the Lord God. Nimrod and his fellows determined to erect the tower of Babel, but ere their task was accomplished God frustrated their plans. Jacob was the child to whom the inheritance was promised, and though Isaac sought to reverse Jehovah's decree and bestow the blessing upon Esau, his efforts came to naught. Esau swore vengeance upon Jacob, but when next they met they wept for joy instead of fighting in hate. The brethren of Joseph determined his destruction, but their evil counsels were overthrown. Pharaoh refused to let Israel carry out the instructions of Jehovah, and perished in the Red Sea for his pains. Balak hired Balaam to curse the Israelites, but God *compelled* him to bless them. Haman erected a gallows for Mordecai but was hanged upon it himself.   Jonah resisted the revealed will of God, but what became of his efforts?

Ah, the heathen may "rage" and the people imagine a "vain thing"; the kings of the earth may "set themselves," and the rulers take counsel together *against* the Lord and against His Christ, saying, " Let us break Their bands asunder, and cast away Their cords from us " (Ps. 2: 1-3).   But is the great God perturbed or disturbed by the rebellion of His puny creatures? No, indeed: " He that sitteth in the heavens shall *laugh*: the Lord shall have them *in derision*" (ver. 4). He is infinitely exalted above all, and the greatest confederacies of earth's pawns, and their most extensive and vigorous preparations to defeat His purpose are, in *His* sight, altogether puerile. He looks upon their puny efforts, not only without any alarm, but He " laughs " at their folly; He treats their impotency with " derision." He knows that He can crush them like moths when He pleases, or consume them in a moment with the breath of His mouth.   Ah, it is but " a *vain* thing " for the potsherds of the earth to strive with the glorious Majesty of Heaven. Such is our God; worship ye Him.

4. GOD GOVERNS ANGELS: BOTH GOOD AND EVIL ANGELS.

The angels are God's servants, His messengers, His chariots. They ever hearken to the word of His mouth and do His commands. " And God *sent* an angel unto Jerusalem to destroy it: and as he was destroying, the Lord beheld, and He repented Him of the evil, and said to the angel that destroyed, It is enough, Stay now thine hand. . . . And the Lord commanded the angel; *and he put his sword* again into the sheath thereof " (1 Chron. 21: 15, 27). Many other scriptures might be cited to show that the angels are in subjection to the will of their Creator and perform His bidding—" And when Peter was come to himself, he said, Now I know of a surety, that the Lord *hath sent His angel*, and hath delivered me out of the hand of Herod " (Acts 12: 11). " And the Lord God of the holy prophets *sent His angel* to shew unto His servants the things which must shortly be done " (Rev. 22: 6).

So it will be when our Lord returns: "The Son of Man shall *send forth His angels* and they shall gather out of His kingdom all things that offend, and them which do iniquity" (Matt. 13:41). Again, we read, "He shall *send His angels* with a great sound of a trumpet, and they shall gather together His elect from the four winds, from one end of heaven to the other" (Matt. 24:31).

The same is true of *evil* spirits: they, too, fulfil God's sovereign decrees. An evil spirit is sent by God to stir up rebellion in the camp of Abimelech (Judges 9:23). Another evil spirit He sent to be a lying spirit in the mouth of Ahab's prophets—"Now therefore, behold, *the Lord hath put* a lying spirit in the mouth of all these thy prophets, and the Lord hath spoken evil concerning thee" (1 Kings 22:23). And yet another was sent by the Lord to trouble Saul—"But the Spirit of the Lord departed from Saul, and *an evil spirit from the Lord* troubled him" (1 Sam. 16:14). So, too, in the New Testament: a whole legion of the demons go not out of their victim until the Lord gives them *permission* to enter the herd of swine.

It is clear from Scripture, then, that the angels, good and evil, are under God's control, and willingly or unwillingly carry out God's purpose. Yea, *SATAN himself* is absolutely subject to God's control. When arraigned in Eden, he listened to the awful sentence, but answered not a word. He was *unable* to touch Job until God granted him leave. So, too, he had to gain our Lord's consent before he could "sift" Peter. When Christ commanded him to depart—"Get thee hence, Satan,"—we read, "*Then* the Devil leaveth Him" (Matt. 4:11). And, in the end, he will be cast into the Lake of Fire, which has been prepared for him and his angels.

The Lord God omnipotent reigneth. His government is exercised over inanimate matter, over the brute beasts, over the children of men, over angels good and evil, and over Satan himself. No revolving of a world, no shining of a star, no storm, no movement of a creature, no actions of men, no errands of angels, no deeds of the Devil—*nothing in all the vast universe can come to pass otherwise than God has eter-*

nally purposed.   Here is a foundation for faith.   Here is a resting place for the intellect.   Here is an anchor for the soul, both sure and steadfast.   It is not blind fate, unbridled evil, man or Devil, but the Lord Almighty who is ruling the world, ruling it according to His own good pleasure and for His own eternal glory.

> "Ten thousand ages ere the skies
>   Were into motion brought;
>   All the long years and worlds to come,
>   Stood present to His thought:
>   There's not a sparrow or a worm,
>   But's found in His decrees,
>   He raises monarchs to their throne
>   And sinks them as He please."
>
>   (ISAAC WATTS)

THE SOVEREIGNTY OF GOD IN SALVATION

"O the depth of the riches both of the wisdom and knowledge of God! how unsearchable are His judgments, and His ways past finding out" (ROM. 11:33).

"SALVATION is of the Lord" (Jonah 2:9); but the Lord does not save all. Why not? He *does* save some; then if He saves some, why not others? Is it because they are too sinful and depraved? No; for the apostle wrote, "This is a faithful saying, and worthy of all acceptation, that Christ Jesus came into the world to save sinners; *of whom I am chief*" (1 Tim. 1:15). Therefore, if God saved the "chief" of sinners, none are excluded because of their depravity. Why then does not God save all? Is it because some are too stony-hearted to be won? No; because of the most stony-hearted people of all it is written, that God will yet "take the stony heart out of their flesh, and will give them a heart of flesh" (Ezek. 11:19). Then is it because some are so stubborn, so intractable, so defiant that God is *unable* to woo them to Himself? Before we answer this question let us ask another; let us appeal to the experience of some, at least, of the Lord's people.

Friend, was there not a time when *you* walked in the counsel of the ungodly, stood in the way of sinners, sat in the seat of the scorners, and with them said, "*We will not* have this Man to reign over us" (Luke 19:14)? Was there not a time when *you* "would not come to Christ that you might have life" (John 5:40)? Yea, was there not a time when you mingled *your* voice with those who said unto God, "Depart from us; for we desire not the knowledge of Thy ways. What is the Almighty, that we should serve Him? and what profit should we have, if we pray unto Him?" (Job 21:14, 15)? With shamed face you have to acknowledge *there was*. But how is it that all is now changed? What was it that brought you from haughty self-sufficiency to be a humble suppliant, from one that was at enmity with God to one that is at peace with Him, from lawlessness to subjection, from hatred to love? And, as one " born of the Spirit," you will readily reply, " *By the grace of God* I am what I am " (1 Cor. 15:10). Then do you not see that it is due to no lack of power in God, nor to His refusal to coerce man, that *other rebels* are not saved too? If God was able to subdue *your* will and win *your* heart, and that *without* interfering with your moral responsibility, then is He not able to do the same for others? Assuredly He is. Then how inconsistent, how illogical, how foolish of you, in seeking *to account for* the present course of the wicked and their ultimate fate, to argue that God is *unable* to save them, *that they will not let Him.* Do you say, " But the time came when *I was willing,* willing to receive Christ as my Saviour "? True, but it was *the Lord* who *made* you willing (Ps. 110:3; Phil. 2:13); why then does He not make *all* sinners willing? Why, but for the fact that He is sovereign and does as He pleases! But to return to our opening inquiry.

Why is it that all are not saved, particularly all who hear the Gospel? Do you still answer, Because the majority refuse to believe? Well. that is true, but it is only a part of the truth. It is the truth *from the human side.* But there is a Divine side too, and this side of the truth needs to be stressed or God will be robbed of His glory. The unsaved are lost because they refuse to believe; the others are saved because they believe. But *why* do these others believe? What is it that causes them to put their trust in Christ? Is it because they are more intelligent than their fellows, and quicker to discern their need of salvation? Perish the thought, " *Who maketh thee to differ from another? And what hast thou that thou didst not receive? Now if thou didst receive it, why dost thou glory, as if thou hadst not received it?*" (1 Cor. 4:7). It is God Himself who makes the difference between the elect and the non-elect, for of His own it is written, " And we know that the Son of God is come, *and hath given us an understanding,* that we may know Him that is true " (1 John 5:20).

Faith is God's *gift,* and "all men have not faith" (2 Thess. 3: 2); therefore, we see that God does not bestow this gift upon all. Upon whom then does He bestow this saving favour? And we answer, upon His own elect—"As many as were ordained to eternal life believed" (Acts 13: 48). Hence it is that we read of "the faith of God's elect" (Titus 1: 1). But is God sovereign in the distribution of His favours? *Has He not the right to be?* Are there still some who "murmur against the Good-Man of the house"? Then His own words are sufficient reply—"Is it not lawful for Me *to do what I will with Mine own*?" (Matt. 20: 15). God is sovereign in the bestowal of His gifts, both in the natural and in the spiritual realms. So much then for a general statement, and now to particularize.

1. THE SOVEREIGNTY OF GOD THE FATHER IN SALVATION.

Perhaps the one passage of Scripture which most emphatically of all asserts the absolute sovereignty of God in connection with His determining the destiny of His creatures, is the ninth of Romans. We shall not attempt to review here the entire chapter, but will confine ourselves to verses 21-23— "Hath not the potter power over the clay, of the same lump to make one vessel unto honour, and another unto dishonour? What if God, willing to show His wrath, and to make His power known, endured with much long-suffering the vessels of wrath fitted to destruction: and that He might make known the riches of His glory on the vessels of mercy, which He had afore prepared unto glory?" These verses represent fallen mankind as inert and as impotent as a lump of lifeless clay. This scripture evidences that there is "no difference," in themselves, between the elect and the non-elect: they are clay of "the same lump," which agrees with Eph. 2: 3, where we are told, that all are by *nature* "children of wrath." It teaches us that the ultimate destiny of every individual is decided by the will of God, and blessed it is that such be the case; if it were left to *our* wills, the ultimate destination of us all would be the Lake of Fire. It declares that God Himself *does* make a difference in the respective destinations to which He assigns His creatures, for one vessel is made " *unto* honour and another *unto* dishonour "; some are " vessels of wrath fitted to destruction," others are " vessels of mercy, which He had afore prepared unto glory."

We readily acknowledge that it is very humbling to the proud heart of the creature to behold all mankind in the hand of God as the clay is in the potter's hand, yet this is precisely how the Scriptures of Truth represent the case. In this day of human boasting, intellectual pride, and deifica- tion of man, it needs to be insisted upon that the potter forms his vessels for himself. Let man strive with his Maker as he will, the fact remains that he is nothing more than clay in the Heavenly Potter's hands, and while we know that God will deal justly with His creatures, that the Judge of all the earth *will do right,* nevertheless, He shapes His vessels for His own purpose and according to His own pleasure. God claims the indisputable right to do as He wills with His own.

Not only has God the right to do as He wills with the creatures of His own hands, but *He exercises this right,* and nowhere is that seen more plainly than in His predestinat- ing grace. Before the foundation of the world God made a choice, a selection, an election. Before His omniscient eye stood the whole of Adam's race, and from it He singled out a people and predestinated them " unto the adoption of children," predestinated them " to be conformed to the image of His Son," " ordained " them unto eternal life. Many are the scriptures which set forth this blessed truth, seven of which will now engage our attention.

" As many as were ordained to eternal life believed " (Acts 13 : 48). Every artifice of human ingenuity has been em- ployed to blunt the sharp edge of this scripture and to ex- plain away the obvious meaning of these words, but it has been employed in vain, though nothing will ever be able to reconcile this and similar passages to the mind of the natural man. " As many as were ordained to eternal life believed." Here we learn four things: First, that believing is the con- sequence *and not the cause* of God's decree. Second, that a limited number only are " ordained to eternal life," for if all men without exception were thus ordained by God, then the words "as many as" are a meaningless qualification. Third, that this "ordination" of God is not to mere external privileges but to "eternal life," not to service but to salvation itself. Fourth, that all—"as many as," not one less —who are thus ordained by God to eternal life will most certainly believe.

The comments of the beloved C. H. Spurgeon on the above passage are well worthy of our notice. Said he, "Attempts have been made to prove that these words do not teach predestination, but these attempts so clearly do violence to language that I will not waste time in answering them. . . . I read: 'As many as were ordained to eternal life believed,' and I shall not twist that text but shall glorify the grace of God by ascribing to it every man's faith. . . . Is it not God who gives the disposition to believe? If men are disposed to have eternal life, does not He in every case dispose them? Is it wrong for God to give grace? If it be right for Him to give it, is it wrong for Him to *purpose* to give it? Would you have Him give it by accident? If it is right for Him to purpose to give grace today, it was right for Him to have purposed it before that date—and, since He changes not— from eternity."

"Even so then at this present time also there is a remnant *according to the election of grace*. And if by grace, then is it no more of works: otherwise grace is no more grace. But if it be of works, then is it no more grace: otherwise work is no more work" (Rom. 11:5, 6). The words "Even so" at the beginning of this quotation refer us to the previous verse where we are told, "I have reserved to Myself seven thousand men who have not bowed the knee to Baal." Note particularly the word "reserved." In the days of Elijah there were seven thousand—a small minority—who were Divinely preserved from idolatry and brought to the knowledge of the true God. This preservation and illumination was not from anything in themselves, but solely by God's special influence and agency. How highly favoured such individuals were to be thus "reserved" by God! Now says the apostle, just as there was a "remnant" in Elijah's days "reserved by God," even so there is in this present dispensation.

"A remnant according to the election of grace." Here the *cause* of election is traced back to its source. The basis upon which God elected this "remnant" was not faith foreseen in them, because a choice founded upon the foresight of good works is just as truly made on the ground of *works* as any choice can be, and in such a case, it would not be "*of grace*"; for, says the apostle, "if by grace, then is it no more of works: otherwise grace is no more grace"; which means that grace and works are opposites, they have nothing in common, and will no more mingle than will oil and water. Thus the idea of inherent good foreseen in those chosen, or of anything meritorious performed by them, is rigidly excluded. "A remnant according to the election *of grace*," signifies an unconditional choice resulting from the sovereign favour of God; in a word, it is absolutely a *gratuitous* election.

"For ye see your calling, brethren, how that not many wise men after the flesh, not many mighty, not many noble, are called: But God hath chosen the foolish things of the world to confound the wise; and God hath chosen the weak things of the world to confound the things which are mighty: and base things of the world, and things which are despised, hath God chosen, yea, and things which are not, to bring to nought things that are: that no flesh should glory in His presence" (1 Cor. 1: 26-29). Three times over in this passage reference is made to *God's choice,* and choice necessarily supposes a selection, the taking of some and the leaving of others. The Chooser here is God Himself. The number chosen is defined—"*not many* wise men after the flesh, *not many* mighty, *not many* noble, are called." So much then for *the fact* of God's choice; now mark the *objects* of His choice.

Those spoken of above as chosen of God are "the weak things of the world, base things of the world, and things which are despised." But why? To demonstrate and magnify His grace. God's *ways* as well as His thoughts are utterly at variance with man's. The carnal mind would have supposed that a selection would have been made from the ranks of the opulent and influential, the amiable and cultured, so that Christianity might have won the approval and applause of the world by its pageantry and fleshly glory. Ah! but " that which is highly esteemed among men is abomination in the sight of God " (Luke 16: 15). God chooses the " *base* things." He did so in Old Testament times. The nation which He singled out to be the depository of His holy oracles and the channel through which the promised Seed should come, was not the ancient Egyptians, the imposing Babylonians, nor the highly civilized and cultured Greeks. No; the people upon whom Jehovah set His love and regarded as " the apple of His eye," were the despised Hebrews. So it was when our Lord tabernacled among men. Those whom He took into favoured intimacy with Himself and commissioned to go forth as His ambassadors, were, for the most part, " unlearned " fishermen. So it has been ever since. And the purpose of God's choice, *the raison d'être* of the selection He has made, is, " that no flesh should glory in His presence." There being nothing whatever in the objects of His choice which would entitle them to His special favours, all the praise must be freely ascribed to the exceeding riches of His manifold grace.

" Blessed be the God and Father of our Lord Jesus Christ, who hath blessed us with all spiritual blessings in the heavenlies in Christ: *according as He hath chosen us in Him before the foundation of the world,* that we should be holy and without blame before Him; in love having predestinated us unto the adoption of children by Jesus Christ to Himself, according to the good pleasure of His will. . . . In whom also we have obtained an inheritance, being predestinated according to the purpose of Him who worketh all things after the counsel of His own will " (Eph. 1: 3-5, 11). Here again we are told at what point in time—if time it could be called—God made choice of those who were to be His children by Jesus Christ. It was not after Adam had fallen and plunged his race into sin and wretchedness, but long ere

Adam saw the light, even before the world itself was founded, that God chose us in Christ. Here also we learn the *purpose* which God had before Him in connection with His own elect: it was that they "should be holy and without blame before Him"; it was "unto the adoption of children"; it was that they should "obtain an inheritance." Here also we discover the *motive* which prompted Him. It was "*in love* that He predestinated us unto the adoption of children by Jesus Christ to Himself"—a statement which refutes the oft-made and wicked charge that, for God to decide the eternal destiny of His creatures before they are born, is tyrannical and unjust. Finally, we are informed here, that in this matter He took counsel with none, but that we are "predestinated according to the good pleasure of His will."

"But we are bound to give thanks alway to God for you, brethren beloved of the Lord, *because God hath from the beginning chosen you to salvation* through sanctification of the Spirit and belief of the truth" (2 Thess. 2:13). There are three things here which deserve special attention. First, the fact that we are expressly told that God's elect are "chosen to salvation." Language could not be more explicit. How summarily do these words dispose of the sophistries and equivocations of all who would make election refer to nothing but external privileges or rank in service! It is to "salvation" itself that God hath chosen us. Second, we are warned here that election unto salvation does not disregard the use of appropriate means: salvation is reached through "sanctification of the Spirit and belief of the truth." It is not true that, because God has chosen a certain one to salvation, he will be saved willy-nilly, whether he believes or not: nowhere do the Scriptures so represent it. The same God who predestined the end, also appointed the means; the same God who "chose unto salvation," decreed that His purpose should be realized through the work of the Spirit and belief of the truth. Third, that God has chosen us unto salvation is a profound cause for fervent praise. Note how strongly the apostle expresses this—"*we are bound* to give thanks *alway* to God for you, brethren beloved of the Lord,

because God hath from the beginning chosen you to salvation," etc.   Instead of shrinking back in horror from the doctrine of predestination, the believer, when he sees this blessed
truth as it is unfolded in the Word, discovers a ground for
gratitude and thanksgiving such as nothing else affords, save
the unspeakable gift of the Redeemer Himself.

" Who hath saved us, and called us with an holy calling,
not according to our works, but according to His own purpose and grace, which was given us in Christ Jesus before
the world began " (2 Tim. 1 : 9).   How plain and pointed is
the language of Holy Writ!   It is man who, by his words,
darkeneth counsel.   It is impossible to state the case more
clearly, or strongly, than it is stated here.   Our salvation is
not "according to *our* works "; that is to say, it is not due
to anything in us, nor the rewarding of anything done by
us; instead, it is the result of God's own " purpose and
grace "; and this grace was given us in Christ Jesus before
the world began.   It is by *grace* we are saved, and in the purpose of God this grace was bestowed upon us not only before we saw the light, not only before Adam's fall, but even
before that far distant " beginning " of Genesis 1 : 1.   And
herein lies the unassailable comfort of God's people.   If His
choice has been from eternity it will last to eternity!

" Elect according to the foreknowledge of God the Father,
through sanctification of the Spirit, unto obedience and
sprinkling of the blood of Jesus Christ " (1 Peter 1 : 2).   Here
again, election by the Father precedes the work of the Holy
Spirit in, and the obedience of faith by, those who are saved;
thus taking it entirely off creature ground, and resting it in
the sovereign pleasure of the Almighty.   The " foreknowledge of God the Father " does not here refer to His prescience of all things, but signifies that the saints were all
eternally present in Christ before the mind of God. God did
not " foreknow " that certain ones who heard the Gospel
would believe it *apart from the fact that He had " ordained "
these certain ones to eternal life*.   What God's prescience saw
in all men was, love of sin and hatred of Himself.   The
" foreknowledge " of God *is based upon His own decrees* as

is clear from Acts 2:23—"Him, being delivered by the determinate counsel and foreknowledge of God, ye have taken, and by wicked hands have crucified and slain"—note the order here: first God's "determinate counsel" (His decree), and second His "foreknowledge." So it is again in Rom. 8: 28, 29, "For whom He did foreknow, He also did predestinate to be conformed to the image of His Son," but the first word here, "for," looks back to the preceding verse and the last clause of it reads, "to them who are the called according to His purpose"—these are the ones whom He did "foreknow and predestinate." Finally, it needs to be pointed out that when we read in Scripture of God "knowing" certain people, the word is used in the sense of knowing with approbation and love: "But if any man love God, the same is *known* of Him" (1 Cor. 8:3). To the hypocrites Christ will yet say "I never knew you"—He never loved them. "Elect according to the foreknowledge of God the Father" signifies, then, chosen by Him as the special objects of His approbation and love.

Summarizing the teaching of these seven passages we learn that, God has "ordained to eternal life" certain ones, and that in consequence of His ordination they, in due time, "believe"; that God's ordination to salvation of His own elect, is not due to any good thing in them nor to anything meritorious from them, but solely of His "grace"; that God has designedly selected the most *unlikely* objects to be the recipients of His special favours, in order that "no flesh should glory in His presence"; that God chose His people in Christ before the foundation of the world, not because they were holy, but in order that they "*should be* holy and without blame before him"; that having selected certain ones to salvation, He also decreed the means by which His eternal counsel should be made good; that the very "grace" by which we are saved was, in God's purpose, "given us in Christ Jesus before the world began"; that long before they were actually created, God's elect stood present before His mind, were "foreknown" by Him, i.e., were the definite objects of His eternal love.

Before we turn to the next division of this chapter, a further word is necessary concerning the *subjects* of God's predestinating grace. We go over this ground again because it is at this point that the doctrine of God's sovereignty in predestinating certain ones to salvation is more frequently assaulted. Perverters of this truth invariably seek to find some cause *outside* God's own will, which *moves* Him to bestow salvation on sinners; something or other is attributed to the creature which entitles him to receive mercy at the hands of the Creator. We return then to the question, *Why* did God choose the ones He did?

What was there in the elect themselves which attracted God's heart to them? Was it because of certain virtues they possessed? because they were generous-hearted, sweet-tempered, truth-speaking? in a word, because they were " good," that God chose them? No; for our Lord said, " There is none good but one, that is God " (Matt. 19: 17). Was it because of any good works they had *performed*? No; for it is written, " There is none that doeth good, no, not one " (Rom. 3: 12). Was it because they evidenced an earnestness and zeal in inquiring after God? No; for it is written again, " There is none that seeketh after God " (Rom. 3: 11). Was it because God foresaw they would believe? No; for how can those who are " *dead* in trespasses and sins " believe in Christ? How could God foreknow some men as believers when belief was impossible to them? Scripture declares that we " believe *through grace* " (Acts 18: 27). Faith is God's gift, and apart from this gift none would believe. The *cause* of His choice then lies within Himself and not in the objects of His choice. He chose the ones He did, simply because He chose to choose them.

> "Sons we are by God's election,
> Who in Jesus Christ believe;
> By eternal destination,
> Sovereign grace we now receive,
>   Lord Thy mercy
> Doth both grace and glory give!"
>
> (From *The Gospel Magazine*, 1777)

2. THE SOVEREIGNTY OF GOD THE SON IN SALVATION.

For whom did Christ die? It surely does not need arguing that the Father had an express purpose in giving Him to die, or that God the Son had a definite design before Him in laying down His life—" Known unto God are all His works from the beginning of the world " (Acts 15: 18). What then was the purpose of the Father and the design of the Son? We answer, Christ died for " God's elect."

We are not unmindful of the fact that the *limited design* in the death of Christ has been the subject of much controversy—what great truth revealed in Scripture has not? Nor do we forget that anything which has to do with the person and work of our blessed Lord requires to be handled with the utmost reverence, and that a " Thus saith the Lord " must be given in support of every assertion we make. Our appeal shall be to the Law and to the Testimony.

For whom did Christ die? Who were the ones He intended to redeem by His blood-shedding? Surely the Lord Jesus had some *absolute determination* before Him when He went to the Cross. If He had, then it necessarily follows that the *extent* of that purpose was *limited*, because an *absolute* determination or purpose of God *must be effected*. If the absolute determination of Christ included all mankind, then all mankind would most certainly be saved. To escape this inevitable conclusion many have affirmed that there was no such absolute determination before Christ, that in His death a merely *conditional provision* of salvation has been made for all mankind. The refutation of this assertion is found in the *promises* made by the Father to His Son *before* He went to the Cross, yea, before He became incarnate. The Old Testament Scriptures represent the Father as promising the Son a certain *reward* for His sufferings on behalf of sinners. At this stage we shall confine ourselves to one or two statements recorded in the well-known fifty-third of Isaiah. There we find the Word saying, " When Thou shalt make His soul an offering for sin, He shall see His seed "; " He shall see of the travail of His soul, and shall be satisfied "; and " My righteous Servant shall justify many " (vers. 10 and 11). But here we would pause and ask, How could it be *certain* that Christ *should* " see His seed," and " see of the travail of His soul and be *satisfied*," unless the salvation of certain members of the human race had been *Divinely decreed*, and therefore was sure? How could it be *certain* that Christ *should* " justify many," if no *effectual* provision was made that *any* should receive Him as their Saviour? On the other hand, to insist that the Lord Jesus *did* expressly purpose the salvation of *all mankind*, is to charge Him with that which no intelligent being should be guilty of, namely, to *design* that which by virtue of His omniscience *He knew would never come to pass*. Hence the only alternative left us is that, so far as the pre-determined purpose of His death is concerned, Christ died for the elect only. Summing up in a sentence, which we trust will be intelligible to every reader, we would say, Christ did not die to *make possible* the salvation of all mankind, but to *make certain* the salvation of all that the Father had given to Him. Christ died not simply to render sins pardonable, but " to *put away sin* by the sacrifice of Himself " (Heb. 9: 26).

(1) The *limited design* in the Atonement follows, necessarily, from the eternal choice of the Father of certain ones unto salvation. The Scriptures inform us that, before the Lord became incarnate He said, " Lo, I come, to do *Thy will* O God " (Heb. 10: 7), and after He had become incarnate He declared ," For I came down from heaven, not to do Mine own will, but the will of Him that sent Me " (John 6: 38). If then God had from the beginning chosen certain ones to salvation, then, because the will of Christ was in perfect accord with the will of the Father, He would not seek to *enlarge* upon His election. What we have just said is not merely a plausible deduction of our own, but is in strict harmony with the express teaching of the Word. Again and again our Lord referred to those whom the Father had " given " Him, and concerning whom He was particularly exercised. Said He, " All that the Father giveth Me shall come to Me; and him that cometh to Me I will in no wise

cast out. . . . And this is the Father's will which hath sent
Me, that of all which He hath given Me I should lose nothing, but should raise it up again at the last day " (John 6:
37, 39). And again, " These words spake Jesus, and lifted
up His eyes to heaven, and said, Father, the hour is come;
glorify Thy Son, that Thy Son also may glorify Thee; As
Thou hast given Him power over all flesh, that He should
give eternal life *to as many as Thou hast given Him*. . . . I
have manifested Thy name *unto the men which Thou gavest
Me out of the world*: Thine they were, and Thou gavest
them Me; and they have kept Thy Word. . . . I pray for
them: I pray not for the world, *but for them which Thou
hast given Me*; for they are Thine. . . . Father, I will that
they also, *whom Thou hast given Me,* be with Me where I
am; that they may behold My glory, which Thou has given
Me: for Thou lovedst Me before the foundation of the
world " (John 17: 1, 2, 6, 9, 24). Before the foundation of
the world the Father predestinated a people to be conformed
to the image of His Son, and the death and resurrection of
the Lord Jesus was in order to the carrying out of the Divine
purpose.

(2) The very *nature* of the Atonement evidences that, in
its application to sinners, it was *limited* in the *purpose* of
God. The Atonement of Christ may be considered from
two chief viewpoints—Godward and manward. Godwards,
the Cross-work of Christ was a *propitiation*, an appeasing of
Divine wrath, a satisfaction rendered to Divine justice and
holiness; manwards, it was a *substitution*, the Innocent taking the place of the guilty, the Just dying for the unjust. But
a strict substitution of a Person for persons, and the inflic-
tion upon Him of voluntary sufferings, involve the *definite
recognition* on the part of the Substitute and of the One He
is to propitiate *of the persons for whom He acts*, whose sins
He bears, whose legal obligations He discharges. Furthermore, if the Law-giver accepts the satisfaction which is made
by the Substitute, then those for whom the Substitute acts,
whose place He takes, must necessarily be acquitted. If I
am in debt and unable to discharge it and another comes for-

ward and pays my creditor in full and receives a receipt in acknowledgment, then, in the sight of the law, my creditor no longer has any claim upon me. On the Cross the Lord Jesus gave Himself a ransom, and that it was accepted by God was attested by the empty grave three days later; the question we would here raise is, *For whom* was this ransom offered? If it was offered for all mankind then the debt incurred by every man has been cancelled. If Christ bore in His own body on the tree the sins of all men without exception, then none will perish. If Christ was " made a curse " for all of Adam's race then none will be finally condemned. " Payment God cannot *twice* demand, first at my bleeding Surety's hand and then again at mine." But Christ *did not* discharge the debt of all men without exception, for some there are who will be " cast into prison " (cf. 1 Peter 3: 19 where the same Greek word for " prison " occurs), and they shall " by no means come out thence, till they have *paid* the uttermost farthing," which will never, never be. Christ *did not* bear the sins of all mankind, for some there are who " die *in their sins*" (John 8: 21), and whose " sin remaineth " (John 9: 41). Christ *was not* " made a curse " for all of Adam's race, for some there are to whom He will yet say, " Depart from Me *ye cursed*" (Matt. 25: 41). To say that Christ died for all alike, to say that He became the Substitute and Surety of the whole human race, to say that He suffered on behalf of and in the stead of all mankind, is to say that He " bore the curse for many who are now bearing the curse for themselves; that He suffered punishment for many who are now lifting up their own eyes in Hell, being in torments; that He paid the redemption price for many who shall yet pay in their own eternal anguish ' the wages of sin, which is death '" (G. S. Bishop). But, on the other hand, to say as Scripture says, that Christ was stricken for the transgressions *of God's people,* to say that He gave His life *for the sheep,* to say that He gave His life a ransom *for many, is to* say that He made an atonement which *fully* atones; it is to say He paid a price which actually ransoms; it is to say He was set forth as a propitiation which really propitiates; it is to say He is a Saviour who truly saves.

(3) Closely connected with, and confirmatory of what we have said above, is the teaching of Scripture concerning our Lord's *priesthood*. It is as the great High Priest that Christ now makes intercession. But *for whom* does He intercede? for the whole human race, or only for His own people? The answer furnished by the New Testament to this question is clear as a sunbeam. Our Saviour has entered into heaven itself " now to appear in the presence of God *for us*" (Heb. 9: 24). that is, for those who are " partakers of the heavenly calling " (Heb. 3: 1). And again it is written, " Wherefore He is able also to save them to the uttermost that come unto God by Him, seeing He ever liveth to make intercession *for them*" (Heb. 7: 25). This is in strict accord with the Old Testament type. After slaying the sacrificial animal, Aaron went into the holy of holies as the representative and on behalf of the people of God: it was the names of *Israel's* tribes which were engraven on his breastplate, and it was in *their* interests he appeared before God. Agreeable to this are our Lord's words in John 17: 9—" I pray for them: I pray *not for the world*, but for them which Thou hast given Me; for they are Thine." Another scripture which deserves careful attention in this connection is found in Romans 8. In verse 33 the question is asked, " Who shall lay anything to the *charge of God's elect*?" and then follows the inspired answer—" It is God that justifieth. Who is he that condemneth? It is Christ that died, yea, rather that is risen again, who is even at the right hand of God, who also maketh intercession *for us*." Note particularly that the death and intercession of Christ have one and the same object! As it was in the type so it is with the antitype—expiation and supplication are *co-extensive*. If then Christ intercedes for the elect only, and " not for the world," then He died for them only.

(4) The number of those who share the benefits of Christ's death is determined not only by the *nature* of the Atonement and the *priesthood* of Christ but also by His *power*.

Grant that the One who died upon the cross was God manifest in the flesh, and it follows inevitably that what Christ has purposed that will He perform; that what He has purchased that will He possess; that what He has set His heart upon that will He secure. If the Lord Jesus possesses all power in heaven and earth, then none can successfully resist His will. But it may be said, This is true in the abstract, nevertheless, Christ refuses to exercise this power, inasmuch as He will never *force* anyone to receive Him as Saviour. In one sense that is true, but in another sense it is positively untrue. The salvation of any sinner *is* a matter of Divine power. By nature the sinner is at enmity with God, and naught but Divine power operating within him, can *overcome* this enmity; hence it is written, "No man can come unto Me, *except* the Father which hath sent Me *draw* him" (John 6: 44). It is the Divine power overcoming the sinner's innate enmity which makes him *willing to come* to Christ that he might have life. But this "enmity" is not overcome in all—why? Is it because the enmity is *too strong* to be overcome? Are there some hearts so steeled against Him that Christ is *unable* to gain entrance? To answer in the affirmative is to *deny His omnipotence*. In the final analysis it is not a question of the sinner's willingness or unwillingness, for by nature *all* are *unwilling*. Willingness to come to Christ is the finished product of Divine power operating in the human heart and will, in overcoming man's inherent and chronic "enmity," as it is written, "Thy people shall be willing in the day *of Thy power*" (Ps. 110: 3). To say that Christ is *unable* to win to Himself those who are unwilling is to deny that all power in heaven and earth is His. To say that Christ cannot put forth His power without destroying man's responsibility is a begging of the question here raised, for *He has* put forth His power and made willing those who *have* come to Him, and if He did this without destroying *their* responsibility, why "cannot" He do so with others? If He is able to win the heart of one sinner to Himself, why not that of another? To say, as is usually said, the others *will not let Him* is to impeach His sufficiency. It is a question of *His* will. If the Lord Jesus has decreed, desired, purposed the salvation of all mankind, then the entire human race *will be saved*, or, otherwise, He lacks the power to make good His intentions; and in such a case it could never be said, "He *shall* see of the travail of His soul and be *satisfied*." The issue raised involves the deity of the Saviour, for a *defeated* Saviour cannot be God.

Having reviewed some of the general principles which require us to believe that the death of Christ was *limited* in its design, we turn now to consider some of the explicit statements of Scripture which expressly affirm it. In that wondrous and matchless fifty-third of Isaiah God tells us concerning His Son, "He was taken from prison and from judgment: and who shall declare His generation? for He was cut off out of the land of the living: *for the transgression of My people was He stricken*" (ver. 8). In perfect harmony with this was the word of the angel to Joseph, "Thou shalt call His name Jesus, for He shall save *His people* from their sins" (Matt. 1: 21), i.e. not merely Israel, but all whom the Father had "given" Him. Our Lord Himself declared, "The Son of Man came not to be ministered unto, but to minister, and to give His life a ransom *for many*" (Matt. 20: 28). But why is it said, "for many," if *all without exception* are included? It was "His people" whom He "redeemed" (Luke 1: 68). It was for "the sheep," and not the "goats," that the Good Shepherd gave His life (John 10: 11). It was the "Church of God" which He purchased with His own blood (Acts 20: 28).

If there is one scripture more than any other upon which we should be willing to rest our case it is John 11: 49-52. Here we are told, "And one of them, named Caiaphas, being the high priest that same year, said unto them, Ye know nothing at all, nor consider that it is expedient for us, that one man should die for the people, and that the whole nation perish not. And this spake he not of himself: but being high priest that year, he prophesied that Jesus should die for that nation; and not for that nation only, but that also

He should gather together in one the children of God that were scattered abroad." Here we are told that Caiaphas " prophesied *not of himself,*" that is, like those employed by God in Old Testament times (see 2 Pet. 1 : 21), his prophecy originated not with himself, but he spake as he was moved by the Holy Spirit; thus is the value of his utterance carefully guarded, and the Divine source of this revelation expressly vouched for. Here, too, we are definitely informed that Christ died *for* " that nation," i.e., Israel, and also for the One Body, His Church, for it is into the Church that the children of God—" scattered " among the nations—are now being " gathered together in one." And is it not remarkable that the members of the Church are here called " children of God " even before Christ died, and therefore before He commenced to build His Church! The vast majority of them had not then been born, yet were they regarded as " children of God "; children of God because they had been chosen in Christ before the foundation of the world, and therefore " predestinated *unto the adoption of children* by Jesus Christ to Himself " (Eph. 1 : 4, 5). In like manner, Christ said, " Other sheep *I have* (not " shall have ") which are not of this fold " (John 10: 16).

If ever the real design of the Cross was uppermost in the heart and speech of our blessed Saviour it was during the last week of His earthly ministry. What then do the Scriptures which treat of *this* portion of His ministry record in connection with our present inquiry? They say, " When Jesus knew that His hour was come that He should depart out of this world unto the Father, *having loved His own* which were in the world, He *loved them* unto the end " (John 13: 1). They record His word, " *For their sakes* I sanctify Myself, that they also might be sanctified through the truth " (John 17: 19); which means, that for the sake of His own, those " given " to Him by the Father, He separated Himself unto the death of the Cross. One may well ask, Why such discrimination of terms if Christ died for all men indiscriminately?

Ere closing this section of the chapter we shall consider

briefly a few of those passages which *seem* to teach most strongly an *unlimited* design in the death of Christ. In 2 Cor. 5: 14 we read, " One died *for all*." But that is not all this scripture affirms. If the entire verse and passage from which these words are quoted be carefully examined, it will be found that instead of teaching an unlimited atonement, it emphatically argues a limited design in the death of Christ. The whole verse reads, " For the love of Christ constraineth us; because we thus judge, that if One died for all, then were all dead." It should be pointed out that in the Greek there is the definite article before the last " all," and that the verb here is in the aorist tense, and therefore should read, " We thus judge: that if One died for all, then they all died." The apostle is here drawing a conclusion, as is clear from the words, " we thus judge, that if . . . then were . . ." His meaning is, that those for whom the One died are regarded, *judicially*, as having died too. The next verse goes on to say, " And He died for all, *that* they which live should not henceforth live unto themselves, but unto Him which died *for them*, and rose again." The One not only died but " rose again," and so, too, did the " all " for whom He died, for it is here said they " live." Those for whom a substitute acts are legally regarded as having acted themselves. In the sight of the law the substitute and those whom he represents are one. So it is in the sight of God. Christ was identified *with His people* and His people were identified with Him, hence when He died they died (judicially) and when He rose they rose also. But further we are told in this passage (ver. 17), that if any man be in Christ he is a new creation; he has received a new life in fact as well as in the sight of the law, hence the " all " for whom Christ died are here bidden to live henceforth no more unto themselves, " but unto Him which died for them, and rose again." In other words, those who belong to this " all " for whom Christ died, are here exhorted to manifest practically in their daily lives what is true of them judicially: they are to " live unto Christ who died *for them*." Thus the " One died *for all* " is defined for us. The " all " for which Christ died are the " they which

live," and which are here bidden to live "unto Him."
This passage then teaches three important truths, and the
better to show its scope we mention them in their inverse
order: certain ones are here bidden to live no more unto
themselves but unto Christ; the ones thus admonished are
"they which live," that is live spiritually, hence, the children
of God, for they alone of mankind possess spiritual life, all
others being *dead* in trespasses and sins; those who *do* thus
live are the ones, the "all," the "them," for whom Christ
died and rose again. This passage therefore teaches that
Christ died for *all His people*, the elect, those given to Him
by the Father; that as the result of His death (and rising
again "*for them*") they "live"—and the elect are the *only*
ones who do thus "live"; and this life which is theirs
through Christ must be lived "unto Him"; Christ's *love*
must now "constrain" them.

"For there is one God, and one Mediator, between God
and men (not "man," for this would have been a generic
term and signified mankind. O the accuracy of Holy Writ!),
the Man Christ Jesus; who gave Himself *a ransom for all*,
to be testified in due time" (1 Tim. 2: 5, 6). It is upon the
words "who gave Himself a ransom for all" we would now
comment. In Scripture the word "all" (as applied to hu-
mankind) is used in two senses—absolutely, and relatively.
In some passages it means *all without exception*; in others
it signifies *all without distinction*. Which of these meanings
it bears in any particular passage must be determined by the
context and decided by a comparison of parallel scriptures.
That the word "all" *is* used in a *relative and restricted*
sense, and in such case means all without distinction and *not*
all without exception, *is* clear from a number of scriptures,
from which we select two or three as samples. "And there
went out unto him all the land of Judea, and they of Jerusalem, and were *all* baptized of him in the river of Jordan,
confessing their sins" (Mark 1: 5). Does this mean that
every man, woman and child from "*all* the land of Judea
and they of Jerusalem" was baptized of John in Jordan?
Surely not. Luke 7: 30 distinctly says, "But the Pharisees

and lawyers rejected the counsel of God against themselves, *being not baptized of him.*" Then what does "*all* baptized of him" mean? We answer it *does not mean* all without exception, *but* all without distinction, that is, all classes and conditions of men. The same explanation applies to Luke 3:21. Again we read, "And early in the morning He came again into the Temple, and *all the people* came unto Him; and He sat down, and taught them" (John 8:2); are we to understand this expression absolutely or relatively? Does "all the people" mean all without exception, or all without distinction, that is, all classes and conditions of people? Manifestly the latter; for the Temple was not able to accommodate *everybody* that was in Jerusalem at this time, namely, the Feast of Tabernacles. Again, we read in Acts 22:15, "For thou (Paul) shalt be His witness *unto all men* of what thou hast seen and heard." Surely "all men" here does not mean every member of the human race. Now we submit that the words "who gave Himself a ransom *for all*" in 1 Tim. 2:6 mean all without distinction, and *not* all without exception. He gave Himself a ransom for men of all nationalities, of all generations, of all classes; in a word, for all the elect, as we read in Rev. 5:9, "For Thou wast slain, and hast redeemed us to God by Thy blood *out of every* kindred, and tongue, and people, and nation." That this is not an *arbitrary* definition of the "all" in our passage is clear from Matt. 20:28 where we read, "The Son of Man came not to be ministered unto, but to minister, and to give His life a *ransom for many,*" which limitation would be quite meaningless if He gave Himself a ransom for all without exception. Furthermore, the qualifying words here, "to be testified in due time," must be taken into consideration. If Christ gave Himself a ransom for the whole human race, in what sense will this be "*testified* in due time" seeing that multitudes of men will certainly be eternally lost? But if our text means that Christ gave Himself a ransom for God's elect, for all without distinction, without distinction of nationality, social prestige, moral character, age or sex, then the meaning of these qualifying words is quite intelligible, for in "due time" this *will be* "testified" in the actual and accomplished salvation of *every one of them*.[1]

"But we see Jesus, who was made a little lower than the angels for the suffering of death, crowned with glory and honour; that He by the grace of God should *taste death for every man*" (Heb. 2:9). This passage need not detain us long. There is no word whatever in the Greek corresponding to "man" in our English version. In the Greek it is left in the abstract—"He tasted death for every." The Revised Version has correctly *omitted* "man" from the text, but has wrongly inserted it in italics. Others suppose the word "thing" should be supplied—"He tasted death for every thing"—but this, too, we deem a mistake. It seems to us that the words which immediately follow explain our text: "*For* it became Him, for whom are all things, and by whom are all things, in bringing many sons unto glory, to make the captain of their salvation perfect through sufferings." It is of "*sons*" the apostle is here writing, and we suggest an *ellipsis* of "son"—thus: "He tasted death for every"—and supply *son* in italics. Thus instead of teaching the unlimited design of Christ's death, Heb. 2:9-10 is in perfect accord with the other scriptures we have quoted which set forth the *restricted* purpose in the Atonement: it was for the "sons" and not the human race our Lord "tasted death."

In closing this section of the chapter let us say that the only limitation in the Atonement we have contended for arises from pure *sovereignty*; it is a limitation not of value and virtue, but of *design* and *application*.[2] We turn now to consider—

3. THE SOVEREIGNTY OF GOD THE HOLY SPIRIT IN SALVATION.

Since the Holy Spirit is one of the three Persons in the blessed Trinity, it necessarily follows that He is in full sym-

---

[1] For another interpretation of this text see *Timothy and Titus*, by William Hendriksen (Banner of Truth, 1960).

[2] For further study see *Redemption—Accomplished and Applied*, by John Murray (Banner of Truth, 1961), and *The Death of Death*, by John Owen (Banner of Truth, 1959).

pathy with the will and design of the other Persons of the Godhead. The eternal *purpose* of the Father in election, the *limited design* in the death of the Son, and the *restricted scope* of the Holy Spirit's operations are in perfect accord. If the Father chose certain ones before the foundation of the world and gave them to His Son, and if it was for them that Christ gave Himself a ransom, then the Holy Spirit is not now working to " bring the world to Christ." The mission of the Holy Spirit *in* the world today is to *apply* the benefits of Christ's redemptive sacrifice. The question which is now to engage us is not the *extent* of the Holy Spirit's *power*— on that point there can be no doubt, it is infinite—but what we shall seek to show is that His power and operations are *directed* by Divine wisdom and sovereignty.

We have just said that the power and operations of the Holy Spirit are directed by Divine wisdom and indisputable sovereignty. In proof of this assertion we appeal first to our Lord's words to Nicodemus in John 3 : 8 : —" The wind bloweth where it listeth, and thou hearest the sound thereof, but canst not tell whence it cometh, and whither it goeth; so is every one that is born of the Spirit." A comparison is here drawn between the wind and the Spirit. The comparison is a *double* one: first, both *are sovereign in their actions*, and second, both are *mysterious in their operations*. The comparison is pointed out in the word " so." The first point of analogy is seen in the words " where it listeth " or " pleaseth "; the second is found in the words " canst not tell." With the second point of analogy we are not now concerned, but upon the first we would comment further.

" The wind bloweth *where it pleaseth* . . . *so* is every one that is born *of the Spirit*." The wind is an element which man can neither harness nor hinder. The wind neither consults man's pleasure nor can it be regulated by his devices. So it is with the Spirit. The wind blows when it pleases, where it pleases, as it pleases. So it is with the Spirit. The wind is regulated by Divine wisdom, yet so far as man is concerned, it is absolutely *sovereign* in its operations. So it is with the Spirit. Sometimes the wind blows so softly it scarcely rustles a leaf; at other times it blows so loudly that its roar can be heard for miles. So it is in the matter of the new birth; with some the Holy Spirit deals so gently, that His work is imperceptible to human onlookers; with others His action is so powerful, radical, revolutionary, that His operations are patent to many. Sometimes the wind is purely local in its reach, at other times wide-spread in its scope. So it is with the Spirit: today He acts on one or two souls, tomorrow He may, as at Pentecost, " prick in the heart " a whole multitude. But whether He works on few or many, He consults not man. He acts *as He pleases.* The new birth is due to *the sovereign will* of the Spirit.

Each of the three Persons in the blessed Trinity is concerned with our salvation: with the Father it is predestination; with the Son propitiation; with the Spirit regeneration. The Father chose us; the Son died for us; the Spirit quickens us. The Father was concerned *about* us; the Son shed His blood *for* us, the Spirit performs His work *within* us. It is with the work of the Spirit we are now concerned, with His work in the new birth, and particularly His *sovereign operations* in the new birth. The Father purposed our new birth; the Son has made possible (by His " travail ") the new birth; but it is the Spirit who *effects* the new birth—" Born *of the Spirit* " (John 3: 6).

The new birth is solely the work of God the Spirit and man has no part or lot in causing it. This from the very nature of the case. Birth altogether excludes the idea of any effort or work on the part of the one who is born. Personally we have no more to do with our spiritual birth than we had with our natural birth. The new birth is a spiritual resurrection, a " passing from death unto life " (John 5:24), and clearly, resurrection is altogether *outside* of man's province. No corpse can re-animate itself. Hence it is written, " It is the Spirit that quickeneth; the flesh profiteth *nothing* " (John 6: 63). But the Spirit does not " quicken " everybody —why? The usual answer returned to this question is, Because everybody does not trust in Christ. It is supposed that the Holy Spirit quickens only those who believe. But this is to put the cart before the horse. Faith is not the cause of the new birth, but the consequence of it. This ought not to need arguing. Faith (in God) is an exotic, something that is not native to the human heart. If faith *were* a natural product of the human heart, the exercise of a principle common to human nature, it would never have been written, " All men have not faith " (2 Thess. 3: 2). Faith is a spiritual grace, the fruit of the spiritual nature, and because the unregenerate are spiritually dead—" dead in trespasses and sins "—then it follows that faith from them is impossible, for a dead man cannot believe anything. " So then they that are in the flesh cannot please God " (Rom. 8: 8)—but they *could* if it were possible for the flesh to believe. Compare with this last-quoted scripture Heb. 11: 6—" But without faith it is impossible to please Him." Can God be " pleased " or satisfied with any thing which does not have its origin in Himself?

That the work of the Holy Spirit *precedes* our believing is unequivocally established by 2 Thess. 2: 13—" God hath from the beginning chosen you to salvation through sanctification of the Spirit and belief of the truth." Note that " sanctification of the Spirit " comes before and makes possible " belief of the truth." What then is the " sanctification of the Spirit"? We answer, *the new birth*. In Scripture " sanctification " *always* means " separation," separation from something and unto something or someone. Let us now amplify our assertion that the " sanctification of the Spirit " corresponds to the new birth and points to the positional effect of it.

Here is a servant of God who preaches the Gospel to a congregation in which are an hundred unsaved people. He brings before them the teaching of Scripture concerning their ruined and lost condition; he speaks of God, His character and righteous demands; he tells of Christ meeting God's demands, and dying the Just for the unjust, and declares that through " this Man " is now preached the forgiveness of sins; he closes by urging the lost to believe what God has said in His Word and receive His Son as their own per-

sonal Saviour. The meeting is over; the congregation dis-
perses; ninety-nine of the unsaved have refused to come to
Christ that they might have life, and go out into the night
having no hope, and without God in the world. But the
hundredth hears the Word of life; the Seed sown falls into
ground which has been prepared by God; he believes the
Good News, and goes home rejoicing that his name is written
in heaven. He has been "born again," and just as a newly-
born babe in the natural world begins life by clinging in-
stinctively, in its helplessness, to its mother, so this new-born
soul has clung to Christ. Just as we read, "The Lord
opened" the heart of Lydia "*that* she attended unto the
things which were spoken of Paul" (Acts 16: 14), so in the
case supposed above, the Holy Spirit quickened that one
before he believed the Gospel message.[1] Here then is the
"sanctification of the Spirit": this one soul who has been
born again has, by virtue of his new birth, been *separated*
from the other ninety-nine. Those born again are, by the
Spirit, *set apart* from those who are *dead* in trespasses and
sins.

To return to 2 Thess. 2: 13: "But we are bound to give
thanks alway to God for you, brethren beloved of the Lord,
because God hath from the beginning chosen you to salvation through sanctification of the Spirit and belief of the
truth." The *order* of thought here is most important and
instructive. First, God's eternal choice; second, the sanctification of the Spirit; third, belief of the truth. Precisely the
same order is found in 1 Pet. 1: 2—"Elect according to the
foreknowledge of God the Father, through sanctification of

[1] The *priority* contended for above is rather in order of nature than
of time, just as the effect *must* ever be preceded by the cause. A
blind man must have his eyes opened before he can see, and yet there
is *no interval* of time between the one and the other. As soon as his
eyes are opened, he sees. So a man must be born again *before* he can
"see the kingdom of God" (John 3:3). *Seeing* the Son is necessary
to believing in Him. Unbelief is attributed to spiritual *blindness*—
those who believed not the "report" of the Gospel "saw no beauty"
in Christ that they should desire Him. The work of the Spirit in
"quickening" the one dead in sins, *precedes* faith in Christ, just as
cause ever precedes effect. But no sooner *is* the heart turned toward
Christ by the Spirit, than the Saviour is embraced by the sinner.

the Spirit, unto obedience and sprinkling of the blood of Jesus Christ." We take it that the "obedience" here is the "obedience of faith" (Rom. 1:5), which appropriates the virtues of the sprinkled blood of the Lord Jesus. So then *before* the "obedience" (of faith, cf. Heb. 5:9), there is the work of the Spirit setting us apart, and behind that is the election of God the Father. The ones "sanctified of the Spirit" then, are they whom "God hath from the beginning His chosen to salvation" (2 Thess. 2:13), those who are "elect according to the foreknowledge of God the Father" (1 Pet. 1:2).

The Holy Spirit is sovereign in His operations and His saving mission is confined to God's elect: they are the ones He "comforts," "seals," guides into all truth, and shews things to come.[1] The work of the Spirit is *necessary* to the complete accomplishment of the Father's eternal purpose. To speak hypothetically but reverently, if God had done nothing more than given Christ to die for sinners, not a single sinner would ever have been saved. In order for any sinner to see his *need* of a Saviour and be willing to *receive* the Saviour he needs, the work of the Holy Spirit upon and within him is imperatively required. Had God done nothing more than given Christ to die for sinners and then sent forth His servants to proclaim salvation through Christ, leaving sinners entirely to themselves to accept or reject as *they* pleased, then *every* sinner would have *rejected*, because at heart every man hates God and is at enmity with Him (Rom. 8:7). Therefore the work of the Holy Spirit is needed to bring the sinner to Christ, to overcome his innate opposi-

---

[1] This is not to deny that the Spirit does work in a certain sense on those who remain unbelievers and finally perish. The Spirit may "*strive*" with the impenitent (Gen. 6:3) and men may resist His operations (Acts 7:51, 52). There is a general work of the Holy Spirit upon those who hear the truth and which in some cases *appears* to be saving (cf. Matt. 13:5, 6, 20, 21) and yet because of the unremoved enmity of the natural heart this work is ineffectual. And as all men are at enmity against God, the Spirit's work would be ineffectual in all if He did not work in a special and regenerating manner in the elect, enabling them to believe those saving truths which " the natural man receiveth not." (1 Cor. 2:14.)—The Publishers.

tion, and bring him to accept the provision God has made. By nature, God's elect are children of wrath *even as others* (Eph. 2 : 3), and as such their hearts are at enmity with God. But this " enmity " of theirs is overcome by the Spirit and it is in consequence of His regenerating work that they believe on Christ. Is it not clear then that the reason why *others* are left outside the kingdom of God, is not only because they are *unwilling* to go in, but also because the Holy Spirit has not so dealt with them? Is it not manifest that the Holy Spirit is *sovereign* in the exercise of His power, that as the wind " bloweth *where it pleaseth*," so the Holy Spirit *operates where He pleases*?

And now to sum up. We have sought to show the perfect consistency of God's ways: that each Person in the Godhead acts in sympathy and harmony with the Others. God the Father elected certain ones to salvation, God the Son died for the elect, and God the Spirit quickens the elect. Well may we sing,

"Praise God from whom all blessings flow,
Praise Him all creatures here below,
Praise Him above ye heavenly host,
Praise Father, Son, and Holy Ghost."

THE SOVEREIGNTY OF GOD IN OPERATION

" For of Him, and through Him, and to Him, *are all things*:
to whom be glory for ever. Amen " (ROM. 11 : 36).

HAS God fore-ordained everything that comes to pass?
Has He decreed that what is, was to have been? In the
final analysis this is only another way of asking, Is God now
governing the world and everyone and everything in it? If
God *is* governing the world, then is He governing it according to a definite purpose, or aimlessly and at random? If
He is governing it according to some purpose, then when
was that purpose made? Is God continually changing His
purpose and making a new one every day, or was His purpose formed from the beginning? Are God's actions, like
ours, regulated by the change of circumstances, or are they
the outcome of His eternal purpose? If God formed a purpose before man was created, then is that purpose going to
be executed according to His original designs and is He now
working towards that end? What saith the Scriptures? They
speak of God as One " who worketh *all things* after the
counsel of His own will " (Eph. 1 : 11).

Few who read this book are likely to call into question the
statement that God knows and foreknows *all things*, but perhaps many would hesitate to go further than this. Yet is it
not self-evident that if God *foreknows* all things, He has also
fore-ordained all things? Is it not clear that God foreknows
what will be *because He has decreed what shall be*? God's
foreknowledge is not the *cause* of events, rather are events
the effects of His eternal purpose. When God has decreed
a thing *shall* be, He *knows* it will be. In the nature of
things there cannot be anything known as what shall be, unless it is *certain* to be, and there is nothing certain to be unless God has *ordained* it shall be. Take the Crucifixion as
an illustration. On this point the teaching of Scripture is

as clear as a sunbeam. Christ as the Lamb whose blood was to be shed, was "foreordained before the foundation of the world" (1 Pet. 1:20). Having then "ordained" the slaying of the Lamb, God *knew* He would be "led to the slaughter," and therefore made it known accordingly through Isaiah the prophet. The Lord Jesus was not "delivered" up by God foreknowing it before it took place, but by His fixed counsel and fore-ordination (Acts 2:23). Foreknowledge of future events then is founded upon God's decrees, hence if God foreknows everything that is to be, it is because He has determined in Himself from all eternity everything which will be—"Known unto God are all His works from the beginning of the world" (Acts 15:18), which shows that God *has a plan*, that God did not begin His work at random or without a knowledge of how His plan would succeed.

God created all things. This truth no one who bows to the testimony of Holy Writ will question; nor would any such be prepared to argue that the work of creation was an *accidental* work. God first formed the purpose to create, and then put forth the creative act in fulfilment of that purpose. All real Christians will readily adopt the words of the Psalmist and say, "O Lord, how manifold are Thy works! *in wisdom* hast Thou made them all." Will any who endorse what we have just said, deny that God purposed to *govern* the world which He created? Surely the creation of the world was not *the end* of God's purpose concerning it. Surely He did not determine simply to create the world and place man in it, and then leave both to their fortunes. It must be apparent that God has some great end or ends in view worthy of His infinite perfections, and that He is now governing the world so as to accomplish these ends—"The counsel of the Lord standeth for ever, the thoughts of His heart to all generations" (Ps. 33:11).

"Remember the former things of old: for I am God, and there is none else; I am God, and there is none like Me, declaring the end from the beginning, and from ancient times the things that are not yet done, saying, My counsel shall stand, and I will do all My pleasure" (Isa. 46:9, 10). Many other passages might be adduced to show that God has many counsels concerning this world and concerning man, and that these counsels will most surely be realized. It is only when they are thus regarded that we can intelligently appreciate the prophecies of Scripture. In prophecy the mighty God has condescended to take us into the secret chamber of His eternal counsels, and make known to us what He has proposed to do in the future. The hundreds of prophecies which are found in the Old and New Testaments are not so much predictions of what *will* come to pass, as they are *revelations to us of what God has purposed SHALL come to pass*. Do we know from prophecy that this present age, like all preceding ones, is to end with a full demonstration of man's failure? Do we know that there is to be a universal turning away from the truth, a general apostasy? Do we know that the Antichrist is to be manifested, and that he will succeed in deceiving the whole world? Do we know that Anti-christ's career will be cut short, and an end made of man's miserable attempts to govern himself, by the return of God's Son? Then it is all because these and a hundred other things are included among God's eternal decrees, now made known to us in the sure Word of Prophecy, and because it is infallibly certain that *all* God has purposed must inevitably come to pass.

What then was the great purpose for which this world and the human race were created? The answer of Scripture is, "The Lord hath made all things *for Himself*" (Prov. 16: 4). And again, "Thou hast created all things, and *for Thy pleasure* they are and were created" (Rev. 4: 11). The great end of creation was the manifestation of God's glory. The heavens declare the glory of God and the firmament sheweth His handiwork; but it was by *man*, originally made in His own image and likeness, that God designed chiefly to manifest His glory. But how was the great Creator to be glorified by man? Before his creation, God foresaw the fall of Adam and the consequent ruin of his race; therefore He could not have designed that man should glorify Him by continuing in a state of innocency. Accordingly, we are taught that

Christ was "fore-ordained before the foundation of the world" to be the Saviour of fallen men. The redemption of sinners by Christ was no mere after-thought of God: it was no expediency to meet an unlooked-for calamity. No; it was a Divine *pro-vision*, and therefore, when man fell, he found mercy walking hand in hand with justice.

From all eternity God designed that our world should be the stage on which He would display His manifold grace and wisdom in the redemption of lost sinners: "To the intent that now unto the principalities and powers in heavenly places might be known by the Church the manifold wisdom of God, according *to the eternal purpose* which He purposed in Christ Jesus our Lord" (Eph. 3: 11). For the accomplishment of this glorious design God has governed the world from the beginning, and will continue to do so to the end. It has been well said, "We can never understand the providence of God over our world, unless we regard it as a complicated machine having ten thousand parts, directed in all its operations to one glorious end—*the display of the manifold wisdom of God in the salvation of the Church*," i.e., the "called out" ones. Everything else down here is subordinated to this central purpose. Apprehending this basic truth, the apostle, moved by the Holy Spirit, was led to write, "Wherefore I endure all things for *the elect's sake,* that *they* may also obtain the salvation which is in Christ Jesus with eternal glory" (2 Tim. 2: 10). What we would now contemplate is *the operation* of God's sovereignty in the government of this world.

In regard to the operation of God's government over the *material* world little need now be said. In previous chapters we have shown that inanimate matter and all irrational creatures are absolutely subject to their Creator's pleasure. While we freely admit that the material world appears to be governed by laws that are stable and more or less uniform in their operations, yet Scripture, history, and observation, compel us to recognize the fact that God suspends these laws, and acts apart from them, whenever it pleases Him to do so. In sending His blessings or judgments upon His creatures He may cause the sun itself to stand still (Josh. 10: 12-13), and the stars in their courses to fight for His people (Judges 5: 20); He may send or withhold " the early and the latter rains " according to the dictates of His own infinite wisdom; He may smite with plague or bless with health; in short, being God and absolute Sovereign, He is bound and tied by no laws of Nature, but governs the material world as seemeth Him best.

But what of God's government of *the human family*? What does Scripture reveal in regard to the *modus operandi* of His governmental administration over mankind? To what extent and by what influences does God control the sons of men? We shall divide our answer to this question into two parts and consider first God's method of dealing with the righteous, His elect; and then His method of dealing with the wicked.

GOD'S METHOD OF DEALING WITH THE RIGHTEOUS:

1. God exerts upon His own elect a *quickening* influence or power.

By nature they are spiritually dead, dead in trespasses and sins, and their first need is spiritual life, for " Except a man be born again, *he cannot* see the kingdom of God " (John 3: 3). In the new birth God brings us from death unto life (John 5: 24). He imparts to us His own nature (2 Pet. 1: 4). He delivers us from the power of darkness and translates us into the kingdom of His dear Son (Col. 1: 13). Now, manifestly, we could not do this ourselves, for we are " without strength " (Rom. 5: 6); hence it is written, " we are *His workmanship* created in Christ Jesus " (Eph. 2: 10).

In the new birth we are made partakers of the Divine nature: a principle, a " seed," a life, is communicated to us, which is " born of the Spirit," and therefore " *is* spirit "; being born of the Holy Spirit, it *is holy*. Apart from this Divine and holy nature which is imparted to us at the new birth, it is utterly impossible for any man to generate a spiritual impulse, form a spiritual concept, think a spiritual thought, understand spiritual things, still less engage in spiritual works. "Without holiness no man shall see the Lord," but the natural man has no desire for holiness, and the provision that God has made he does not want. Will then a man pray for, seek for, strive after, that which he dislikes? Surely not. If then a man *does* "follow after" that which by nature he cordially dislikes, if he does now love the One he once hated, it is because a miraculous change has taken place within him; a power outside of himself has operated upon him, a nature entirely different from his old one has been imparted to him, and hence it is written, "Therefore if any man be in Christ, *he is a new creation*: old things are passed away, behold all things are become new" (2 Cor. 5: 17). Such an one as we have just described has passed from death unto life, has been turned from darkness to light, and from the power of Satan unto God (Acts 26: 18). In no other way can the great change be accounted for.

The new birth is very much more than simply shedding a few tears due to a temporary remorse over sin. It is far more than changing our course of life, the leaving off of bad habits and the substituting of good ones. It is something different from the mere cherishing and practising of noble ideals. It goes infinitely deeper than coming forward to take some popular evangelist by the hand, signing a pledge-card, or "joining the church." The new birth is no mere turning over a new leaf, but is the inception and reception of a new life. It is no mere reformation but a complete transformation. In short, the new birth is a miracle, the result of the supernatural operation of God. It is radical, revolutionary, lasting.

Here then is the first thing, in time, which God does in His own elect. He lays hold of those who are spiritually dead and quickens them into newness of life. He takes up one who was conceived in sin and shapen in iniquity, and conforms him to the image of His Son. He seizes a captive of the Devil and makes him a member of the household of faith. He picks up a beggar and makes him joint-heir with

Christ. He comes to one who is full of enmity against Him, and gives him a new heart that is full of love for Him. He stoops to one who by nature is a rebel, and works in him both to will and to do of His good pleasure. By His irresistible power He transforms a sinner into a saint, an enemy into a friend, a slave of the Devil into a child of God. Surely then we are moved to say,

> "When all Thy mercies, O my God,
>   My rising soul surveys,
>   Transported with the view, I'm lost
>   In wonder, love and praise."

2. God exerts upon His own elect an *energizing* influence or power.

The apostle prayed to God for the Ephesian saints that the eyes of their understanding might be enlightened, in order that, among other things, they might know " what is the exceeding greatness of His power *to usward who believe*" (Eph. 1:18), and that they might be " strengthened with might by His Spirit in the inner man " (3:16). It is thus that the children of God are enabled to fight the good fight of faith, and battle with the adverse forces which constantly war against them. In themselves they have no strength: they are but "sheep." A sheep is one of the most defenceless animals there is; but the promise is sure—" He giveth power to the faint, and to them that have no might He increaseth strength " (Isa. 40:29).

It is this energizing power that God exerts upon and within the righteous which enables them to serve Him acceptably. Said the prophet of old, " But truly I am full of power *by the Spirit of the Lord*" (Micah 3:8). And said our Lord to His apostles, " Ye shall *receive power* after that the Holy Spirit is come upon you " (Acts 1:8), and thus it proved, for of these same men we read subsequently, " And with great power gave the apostles witness of the resurrection of the Lord Jesus: and great grace was upon them all " (Acts 4:33). So it was, too, with the apostle Paul: " And my speech and my preaching was not with enticing words of man's wisdom, but in demonstration of the Spirit and of power" (1 Cor. 2:4). But the scope of this power is not confined to service, for we read in 2 Pet. 1:3, "According as His Divine power hath given unto us *all things that pertain unto life and godliness,* through the knowledge of Him that hath called us to glory and virtue." Hence it is that the various graces of the Christian character, "love, joy, peace, long-suffering, gentleness, goodness, faith, meekness, temperance," are ascribed directly to God Himself, being denominated "the fruit *of the Spirit*" (Gal. 5:22). Compare 2 Cor. 8:16.

3. God exerts upon His own elect a *directing* influence or power.

Of old He led His people across the wilderness, directing their steps by a pillar of cloud by day and a pillar of fire by night; and today He still directs His saints, though now from within rather than from without. "For this God *is our God* for ever and ever: He will be our *Guide* even unto death" (Ps. 48:14), but He "guides" us by working in us both to will and to do of His good pleasure. That He does so guide us is clear from the words of the apostle in Eph. 2:10—"For we are His workmanship, created in Christ Jesus unto good works, *which God hath before ordained that we should walk in them.*" Thus all ground for boasting is removed, and God gets all the glory, for with the prophet we have to say, "Lord, Thou wilt ordain peace for us: *for Thou also hast wrought all our works in us*" (Isa. 26:12). How true then that "A man's heart deviseth his way: but the Lord *directeth his steps*" (Pro. 16:9)! Compare Ps. 65:4, Ezek. 36:27.

4. God exerts upon His own elect a *preserving* influence or power.

Many are the scriptures which set forth this blessed truth. "He preserveth the souls of His saints; He delivereth them out of the hand of the wicked" (Ps. 97:10). "For the Lord loveth judgment, and forsaketh not His saints; they are *preserved for ever*: but the seed of the wicked shall be cut off"

(Ps. 37: 28). " The Lord preserveth *all* them that love Him: but all the wicked will He destroy " (Ps. 145: 20). It is need-less to multiply texts or to raise an argument at this point respecting the believer's responsibility and faithfulness—we can no more " persevere " *without* God preserving us, than we can breathe when God ceases to give us breath; we are " *kept by the power of God* through faith unto salvation ready to be revealed in the last time " (1 Pet. 1: 5). Compare 1 Chron. 18: 6. It remains for us now to consider,

God's method of dealing with the wicked:

In contemplating God's governmental dealings with the non-elect we find that He exerts upon them a fourfold in-fluence or power. We adopt the clear-cut divisions suggested by Dr. Rice:

1. God sometimes exerts upon the wicked *a restraining* in-fluence by which they are *prevented* from doing what they are naturally inclined to do.

A striking example of this is seen in Abimelech, king of Gerar. Abraham came down to Gerar, and, fearful lest he might be slain on account of his wife, he instructed her to pose as his sister. Regarding her as an unmarried woman, Abimelech sent and took Sarah unto himself; and then we learn how God put forth His power to protect her honour— " And God said unto him in a dream, Yea, I know that thou didst this in the integrity of thy heart; *for I also withheld thee from sinning against Me*: therefore *suffered I thee not to touch her*" (Gen. 20: 6). Had not God interposed, Abime-lech would have grievously wronged Sarah, but the Lord restrained him and did not allow him to carry out the inten-tions of his heart.

A similar instance is found in connection with Joseph and his brethren's treatment of him. Owing to Jacob's partiality for Joseph, his brethren " hated him," and when they thought they had him in their power, " they conspired against him to *slay* him " (Gen. 37: 18). But God did not allow them to carry out their evil designs. First He moved Reuben to deliver him out of their hands, and next he caused Judah to suggest that Joseph should be sold to the passing Ishmaelites, who carried him down to Egypt. That it was *God* who thus restrained them is clear from the words of Joseph himself, when some years later he made himself known to his brethren: said he, "So now it was not you that sent me hither, *but God*" (Gen. 45:8)!

The restraining influence which God exerts upon the wicked was strikingly exemplified in the person of Balaam, the prophet hired by Balak to curse the Israelites. One cannot read the inspired narrative without discovering that, left to himself, Balaam had readily and certainly accepted the offer of Balak. How evidently God restrained the impulses of his heart is seen from his own acknowledgment—" How shall I curse, whom God hath not cursed? or how shall I defy, whom the Lord hath not defied? Behold I have *received commandment* to bless: and He hath blessed; and I cannot reverse it " (Num. 23:8, 20).

Not only does God exert a restraining influence upon wicked individuals, but He does so upon whole peoples as well. A remarkable illustration of this is found in Ex. 34: 24—" For I will cast out the nations before thee, and enlarge thy borders: *neither shall any man desire thy land*, when thou shalt go up to appear before the Lord thy God thrice in the year." Three times a year every male Israelite, at the command of God, left his home and inheritance and journeyed to Jerusalem to keep the Feasts of the Lord; and in the above scripture we learn He promised them that, while they were at Jerusalem, He would guard their unprotected homes by *restraining* the covetous designs and desires of their heathen neighbours.

2. God sometimes exerts upon the wicked a *softening* influence disposing them, contrary to their natural inclinations, to do that which will promote *His* cause.

Above, we referred to Joseph's history as an illustration of God exerting a *restraining* influence upon the wicked; let us note now his experiences in Egypt as exemplifying our assertion that God also exerts a *softening* influence upon the unrighteous. We are told that while he was in the house of Potiphar, " the Lord was with Joseph." His master saw that the Lord was with him, and in consequence, " Joseph found favour in his sight and he made him overseer over his house " (Gen. 39: 3, 4). Later, when Joseph was unjustly cast into prison, we are told, " But the Lord was with Joseph, and shewed him mercy, and *gave him favour in the sight of the keeper of the prison* " (Gen. 39: 21), and in consequence the prison-keeper shewed him much kindness and honour. Finally, after his release from prison, we learn from Acts 7: 10 that the Lord " *gave him favour and wisdom in the sight of Pharaoh king of Egypt*; and he made him governor over Egypt and all his house."

An equally striking evidence of God's power to melt the hearts of his enemies, is seen in Pharaoh's daughter's treatment of the infant Moses. The incident is well known. Pharaoh had issued an edict commanding the destruction of every male child of the Israelites. A certain Levite had a son born to him who for three months was kept hidden by his mother. No longer able to conceal the infant Moses, she placed him in an ark of bulrushes, and laid him by the river's brink. The ark was discovered by none less than the king's daughter who had come down to the river to bathe, but instead of heeding her father's wicked decree and casting the child into the river, we are told that " *she had compassion on him* " (Ex. 2: 6)! Accordingly, the young life was spared, and later Moses became the adopted son of this princess!

God has access to the hearts of all men and He may soften them according to His sovereign purpose. The profane Esau swore vengeance upon his brother for the deception which he had practised upon his father, yet when next he met Jacob, instead of slaying him, Esau " fell on his neck and kissed him " (Gen. 32: 4)! Ahab, the weak and wicked consort of Jezebel, was highly enraged against Elijah the prophet, at whose word the heavens had been shut up for three years and a half: so angry was he against the one whom he regarded as his enemy that he searched for him in every nation and kingdom, and when he could not be found, " he took an oath " (1 Kings 18: 10). Yet, when they met, instead of killing the prophet, Ahab obeyed Elijah's behest and " sent unto all the children of Israel and gathered the prophets together unto Mount Carmel " (ver. 20). Again, Esther the Jewess is about to enter the presence-chamber of the august Medo-Persian monarch which, said she, " is not according to the law " (Est. 4: 16). She went in expecting to " perish," but we are told, " *She obtained favour in his sight,* and the king held out to Esther the golden sceptre " (5 : 2). Yet again; young Daniel is a captive in a foreign court. The king " appointed " a daily provision of meat and drink for Daniel and his fellows. But Daniel purposed in his heart that he would not defile himself with the allotted portion, and accordingly made known his purpose to his master, the prince of the eunuchs. What happened? His master was a heathen, and " feared " the king. Did he turn then upon Daniel and angrily demand that his orders be promptly carried out? No; for we read, " *Now God had brought Daniel into favour and tender love with the prince of the eunuchs*" (Dan. 1: 9)!

" The king's heart is in the hand of the Lord, as the rivers of water: He turneth it whithersoever He will " (Prov. 21: 1). A remarkable illustration of this is seen in Cyrus, the heathen king of Persia. God's people were in captivity, but the predicted end of their captivity was almost reached. Meanwhile the Temple at Jerusalem lay in ruins, and the Jews were in a distant land. What hope was there then that the Lord's house would be re-built? Mark now what God did: " Now in the first year of Cyrus king of Persia, that the word of the Lord by the mouth of Jeremiah might be fulfilled, *the Lord stirred up the spirit of Cyrus* king of Persia, that he made a proclamation throughout all his kingdom, and put it in writing, saying, Thus saith Cyrus king of Persia, The Lord God of heaven hath given me all the kingdoms of the earth; and He hath charged me to build Him an house at Jerusalem, which is in Judah " (Ezra 1: 1, 2). Cyrus, be it remembered, was a pagan, and as secular history bears witness, a very wicked man, yet the Lord moved him to issue this edict, that His Word through Jeremiah seventy years before might be fulfilled. A similar and further illustration is found in Ezra 7:27, where we find Ezra returning thanks for what God had caused king Artaxerxes to do in completing and beautifying the house which Cyrus had commanded to be erected —" Blessed be the Lord God of our fathers *which hath put such a thing as this in the king's heart,* to beautify the house of the Lord which is in Jerusalem " (Ezra 7:27).

3. God sometimes exerts upon the wicked a *directing* influence so that good is made to result from their intended evil.

Once more we revert to the history of Joseph as a case in point. In selling Joseph to the Ishmaelites, his brethren were actuated by cruel and heartless motives. Their object was to make away with him, and the passing of these travelling traders furnished an easy way out for them. To them the act was nothing more than the enslaving of a noble youth for the sake of gain. But now observe how God was secretly working and over-ruling their wicked actions. Providence so ordered it that these Ishmaelites passed by just in time to prevent Joseph being murdered, for his brethren had already taken counsel together to put him to death. Further; these Ishmaelites were journeying to Egypt, which was the very country to which *God* had purposed to send Joseph, and He *ordained* they should purchase Joseph just when they did. That the hand of God was in this incident, that it was something more than a fortunate coincidence, is clear from the words of Joseph to his brethren at a later date, " *God sent me* before you to preserve you a posterity in the earth, and to save your lives by a great deliverance " (Gen. 45:7).

Another equally striking illustration of *God directing the wicked* is found in Isaiah 10:5-7—" O Assyrian, the rod of Mine anger, and the staff in their hand is Mine indignation. *I will send him* against a hypocritical nation, and against the people of My wrath will I give him a charge, to take the spoil, and to take the prey, and to tread them down like the mire of the streets. *Howbeit he meaneth not so, neither doth his heart think so*; but it is in his heart to destroy and cut off nations not a few." Assyria's king had determined to be a world-conqueror, to "cut off nations not a few." But God *directed* and *controlled* his military lust and ambition, and caused him to concentrate his attention at that time on the conquest of the insignificant nation of Israel. Such a task was not in the proud king's heart—" he meant it not so "— but *God* gave him this charge and he could do nothing but fulfil it. Compare also Judges 7 : 22.

The supreme example of the controlling, directing influence which God exerts upon the wicked, is *the Cross of Christ* with all its attendant circumstances. If ever the *superintending* providence of God was witnessed, it was there. From all eternity God had predestined every detail of that event of all events. Nothing was left to chance or the caprice of man. God had decreed when and where and how His blessed Son was to die. Much of what He had purposed concerning the Crucifixion had been made known through the Old Testament prophets, and in the accurate and literal *fulfilment* of these prophecies we have clear proof, full demonstration, of the controlling and directing influence which God exerts upon the wicked. Not a thing occurred except as God had ordained, and *all* that He had ordained took place exactly as He purposed. Had it been decreed (and made known in Scripture) that the Saviour should be betrayed by one of His own disciples—by His "familiar friend"—see Ps. 41 : 9 and compare Matt. 26 : 50? then the disciple Judas is the one who sold Him. Had it been decreed that the betrayer should receive for his awful perfidy thirty pieces of silver? then are the chief priests moved to offer him this very sum. Had it been decreed that this betrayal sum should be put to a particular use, namely, purchase the potter's field? then the hand of God directs Judas to return the money to the chief priests, and so guides their "counsel" (Matt. 27 : 7) that they do this very thing. Had it been decreed that there should be those who bore "false witness" against our

Lord (Ps. 35: 11)? then accordingly such were raised up. Had it been decreed that the Lord of glory should be "spat upon and scourged" (Isa. 50: 6)? then there were not found wanting those who were vile enough to do so. Had it been decreed that the Saviour should be "numbered with the transgressors"? then unknown to himself, Pilate, directed by God, gave orders for His crucifixion along with two thieves. Had it been decreed that vinegar and gall should be given Him to drink while He hung upon the Cross? then this decree of God was executed to the very letter. Had it been decreed that the heartless soldiers should gamble for His garments? then sure enough they did this very thing. Had it been decreed that not a bone of Him should be broken (Ex. 12: 46; Num. 9: 12)? then the controlling hand of God which suffered the Roman soldiers to break the legs of the thieves, prevented them from doing the same with our Lord. Ah! there were not enough soldiers in all the Roman legions, there were not sufficient demons in all the hierarchies of Satan, to break one bone in the body of Christ. And why? Because the Almighty Sovereign had decreed that not a bone *should be* broken. Do we need to extend this paragraph any further? Does not the accurate and literal fulfilment of all that Scripture had predicted in connection with the Crucifixion, demonstrate beyond all controversy that an Almighty power was *directing* and *superintending* everything that was done on that Day of days?

4. God also *hardens* the hearts of wicked men and *blinds* their minds.

"*God* hardens men's hearts! *God* blinds men's minds!" Yes, so Scripture represents Him. In developing this theme of the sovereignty of God in Operation we recognize that we have now reached its most solemn aspect of all, and that here especially, we need to keep very close indeed to the words of Holy Writ. God forbid that we should go one fraction *further* than His Word goes; but may He give us grace to go *as far as* His Word goes. It is true that secret things belong unto the Lord, but it is also true that those things which are revealed in Scripture belong unto us and to our children.

"*He* turned their heart to *hate* His people, to deal *subtly* with His servants" (Ps. 105: 25). The reference here is to the sojourn of the descendants of Jacob in the land of Egypt, when, after the death of the Pharaoh who had welcomed the old patriarch and his family, there " arose up a new king who knew not Joseph." In his days the children of Israel " increased greatly" so that they outnumbered the Egyptians; then it was that God " turned their heart to hate His people."

The consequence of the Egyptians' " hatred" is well known: they brought them into cruel bondage and placed them under merciless taskmasters, until their lot became unendurable. Helpless and wretched, the Israelites cried unto Jehovah, and in response, He appointed Moses to be their deliverer. God revealed Himself unto His chosen servant, gave him a number of miraculous signs which he was to exhibit at the Egyptian court, and then bade him go to Pharaoh, and demand that the Israelites should be allowed to go a three days' journey into the wilderness, that they might worship the Lord. But before Moses started out on his journey God warned him concerning Pharaoh, "*I will harden his heart* that he shall not let the people go " (Ex. 4: 21). If it be asked, *Why* did God harden Pharaoh's heart? the answer furnished by Scripture itself is, In order that God might show forth *His power* in him (Rom. 9: 17); in other words, it was so that the Lord might demonstrate His glory in the overthrow of this haughty and powerful monarch. If it should be pressed further, Why did God *select such a method* of displaying His power? then the answer must be, that being sovereign, God reserves to Himself the right to act as He pleases.

Not only are we told that God hardened the heart of Pharaoh so that he would not let the Israelites go; but after God had plagued his land so severely that he reluctantly gave a qualified permission, and after the first-born of all the Egyptians had been slain, and Israel had actually left the land of bondage, God told Moses, "And I, behold, *I will harden the hearts of the Egyptians*, and they shall follow them: and I will get Me honour upon Pharaoh, upon his chariots, and upon his horsemen. And the Egyptians shall know that I am the Lord, when I have gotten Me honour upon Pharaoh, upon his chariots, and upon his horsemen " (Ex. 14: 17, 18).

The same thing happened subsequently in connection with Sihon, king of Heshbon, through whose territory Israel had to pass on their way to the promised Land. When reviewing their history, Moses told the people, " But Sihon king of Heshbon would not let us pass by him: *for the Lord thy God hardened his spirit, and made his heart obstinate,* that He might deliver him into thy hand " (Deut. 2: 30)!

So it was also after Israel had entered Canaan. We read, " There was not a city that made peace with the children of Israel, save the Hivites the inhabitants of Gibeon: all other they took in battle. *For it was of the Lord to harden their hearts, that they should come against Israel* in battle, that He might destroy them utterly, and that they might have no favour, but that He might destroy them, as the Lord commanded Moses " (Josh 11: 19, 20). From other scriptures we learn why God purposed to " destroy utterly " the Canaanites—it was because of their awful wickedness and corruption.

Nor is the revelation of this solemn truth confined to the Old Testament. In John 12: 37-40 we read, " But though He had done so many miracles before them, yet they believed not on Him: *that* (in order that) *the saying of Isaiah the prophet might be fulfilled,* which he spake, Lord, who hath believed our report? and to whom hath the arm of the Lord been revealed? *Therefore they could not believe,* because that Isaiah said again, *HE hath blinded their eyes, and hardened their heart; that they should not* see with their eyes, nor understand with their heart, and be converted, and I should heal them." It needs to be carefully noted here that those whose eyes God " blinded " and whose heart He " hardened," were men who had deliberately scorned the Light and rejected the testimony of God's own Son.

Similarly we read in 2 Thess. 2: 11, 12, " And for this cause *God shall send them strong delusion*, that they should believe a lie: that they all might be damned who believed not the truth, but had pleasure in unrighteousness." The fulfilment of this scripture is yet future. What God did unto the Jews of old He is yet going to do unto Christendom. Just as the Jews of Christ's day despised His testimony, and in consequence, were " blinded," so a guilty Christendom which has rejected the Truth shall yet have sent them from God a " strong delusion " that they may believe a lie.

Is God really governing the world? Is He exercising rule over the human family? What is the *modus operandi* of His governmental administration over mankind? To what extent and by what means does He control the sons of men? *How* does God exercise an influence upon the wicked, seeing their hearts are at enmity against Him? These are some of the questions we have sought to answer from Scripture in the previous sections of this chapter. Upon His own elect, God exerts a quickening, an energizing, a directing, and a preserving power. Upon the wicked, God exerts a restraining, softening, directing, and hardening, and blinding power, according to the dictates of His own infinite wisdom and justice and unto the outworking of His own eternal purpose. God's decrees *are* being executed. What He has ordained is being accomplished. *Man's wickedness is bounded*. The limits of evil-doing and of evil-doers have been Divinely defined and cannot be exceeded. Though many are in ignorance of it, all men, good and bad, are under the jurisdiction of, and are absolutely subject to the administration of, the Supreme Sovereign—" Alleluia: for the Lord God omnipotent reigneth " (Rev. 19: 6)—reigneth over all !

GOD'S SOVEREIGNTY AND THE HUMAN WILL

"It is God which worketh in you *both to will and to do* of His good pleasure" (PHIL. 2:13).

CONCERNING the nature and the power of fallen man's will, the greatest confusion prevails today and the most erroneous views are held, even by many of God's children. The popular idea now prevailing, and which is taught from the great majority of pulpits, is that man has a "free will," and that salvation comes to the sinner through his *will* co-operating with the Holy Spirit. To deny the "free will" of man, i.e. his power to choose that which is good, his native ability to accept Christ, is to bring one into disfavour at once, even before most of the those who profess to be orthodox. And yet Scripture emphatically says, "*It is not* of him that willeth, nor of him that runneth, but of God that showeth mercy" (Rom. 9:16). Again the Word expressly declares, "There is *none that seeketh* after God" (Rom. 3:11). Did not Christ say to the men of His day, "Ye *will not* come to Me, that ye might have life" (John 5:40)? Yes, but some *did* "come" to Him, some *did* receive Him. True and who were they? John 1:12, 13 tells us: "But as many as received Him, to them gave He power to become the sons of God, even to them that believe on His name: which *were born*, not of blood, *nor of the will* of the flesh, nor of the will of man, but of God"!

But does not Scripture say, "Whosoever will may come"? It does, but does this signify that everybody has the will *to* come? What of those who *won't* come? "Whosoever will may come" no more implies that fallen man has the power in himself *to* come, than "Stretch forth thine hand" implied that the man with the withered arm had ability in himself to comply. In and of himself the natural man has power to reject Christ; but in and of himself he has not the power to receive Christ. And why? Because he has a mind that is "enmity against" Him (Rom. 8:7); because he has a heart that hates Him (John 15:18). Man chooses that which is according to his nature, and therefore before he will ever choose or prefer that which is divine and spiritual, a new nature must be imparted to him; in other words, he *must* be born again.

But it may be asked, Does not the Holy Spirit *overcome* a man's enmity and hatred when He convicts the sinner of his sins and his need of Christ; and does not the Spirit of God produce such conviction in many that perish? Such language betrays confusion of thought: were such a man's enmity *really* "overcome," then he *would* readily turn to Christ; that he does not come to the Saviour, demonstrates that his enmity is not overcome. But that many are, through the preaching of the Word, convicted by the Holy Spirit, who nevertheless die in unbelief, is solemnly true. Yet it is a fact which must not be lost sight of, that the Holy Spirit does *something more* in each of God's elect than He does in the non-elect: He works in them "both to will and to do of God's good pleasure" (Phil. 2:13).

In reply to what we have said above, Arminians would answer, No; the Spirit's work of conviction is the same both in the converted and in the unconverted. That which distinguishes the one class from the other is that the former *yield* to His strivings, whereas the latter resist them. But if this *were* the case, then the Christian would *make himself* to "differ," whereas the Scripture attributes the "differing" to God's discriminating grace (1 Cor. 4:7). Again; if such *were* the case, then the Christian would have ground for boasting and self-glorying over *his* co-operation with the Spirit; but this would flatly contradict Eph. 2:8, "For by grace are ye saved through faith; and that *not of yourselves*: it is the gift of God."

Let us appeal to the actual experience of the Christian reader. Was there not a time (may the remembrance of it bow each of us into the dust!) when you were unwilling to come to Christ? There was. Since then you *have* come to

Him. Are you now prepared to give Him all the glory for that (Ps. 115: 1)? Do you not acknowledge you came to Christ because the Holy Spirit brought you from unwillingness to willingness? You do. Then is it not also a patent fact that the Holy Spirit has not done in many others what He *has* in you? Granted that many others have heard the Gospel, been shown their need of Christ; yet, they are still unwilling to come to Him. Thus He *has* wrought more in you than in them. Do you answer, Yet I remember well the time when the Great Issue was presented to me, and my consciousness testifies that my will acted and that I yielded to the claims of Christ upon me. Quite true! But *before* you " yielded," the Holy Spirit overcame the native enmity of your mind against God, and this " enmity" He does not overcome in all. Should it be said, That is because they are unwilling for their enmity to be overcome—ah, none are thus " willing" till He has put forth His *almighty* power and wrought a miracle of grace in the heart.

But let us now inquire, *What is* the human Will? Is it a self-determining agent, or is it, in turn, determined by something else? Is it sovereign or servant? Is the will superior to every other faculty of our being so that it governs them, or is it moved by their impulses and subject to their pleasure? Does the will rule the mind, or does the mind control the will? Is the will free to do as it pleases, or is it under the necessity of rendering obedience to something outside of itself? " Does the will stand apart from the other great faculties or powers of the soul, *a man within a man,* who can reverse the man and fly against the man and split him into segments, as a glass snake breaks in pieces? Or, is the will connected with the other faculties, as the tail of the serpent is with his body, and that again with his head, so that where the head goes, the whole creature goes, and, as a man *thinketh* in his *heart,* so is he? First, thought; then, heart (desire or aversion); and then act. Is it this way the dog wags the tail? Or, is it the will, the tail, that wags the dog? Is the will the first and chief thing in the man, or is it the last thing—to be kept subordinate, and in its place beneath the other faculties—and, is the true philosophy of moral action and its process that of Gen. 3:6: 'And when the woman saw that the tree was good for food' (sense-perception, intelligence), 'and a tree to be desired' (affections), 'she took and ate thereof' (the will)." (G. S. Bishop). These are questions of more than academic interest. They are of practical importance. We believe that we do not go too far when we affirm that the answer returned to these questions is one of the fundamental tests of doctrinal soundness.[1]

1. THE NATURE OF THE HUMAN WILL.

What is the Will? We answer, the will is the faculty of choice, the immediate cause of all action. Choice necessarily implies the refusal of one thing and the acceptance of another. The positive and the negative must both be present to the mind before there can be any choice. In every act of the will there is preference—the desiring of one thing rather than another. Where there is no preference, but complete indifference, there is no volition. To will is to choose, and to choose is to decide between alternatives. But there is something which *influences* the choice; something which *determines* the decision. Hence the will cannot be sovereign, because it is the servant of that something. The will cannot be both sovereign and servant. It cannot be both cause and effect. The will is *not causative*, because, as we have said, something causes it to *choose;* therefore that something must be the causative agent. Choice itself is affected by certain considerations, is determined by various influences brought to bear *upon the individual himself;* hence, volition is the effect of these considerations and influences, and if the effect, it must be their *servant;* and if the will is their ser-

---

[1] Since writing the above we have read an article by the late J. N. Darby entitled "Man's so-called freewill," that opens with these words: "This re-appearance of the doctrine of freewill serves to support that of the pretension of the natural man to be not irremediably fallen, for this is what such doctrine tends to. All who have never been deeply convicted of sin, all persons in whom this conviction is based on gross external sins, believe more or less in freewill."

vant then it is not sovereign, and if the will is *not* sovereign, we certainly cannot predicate absolute "freedom" of it. Acts of the will cannot come to pass of themselves—to say they can, is to postulate an *uncaused* effect. 'Ex nihilo nihil fit'—out of nothing, nothing comes.

In all ages, however, there have been those who contended for the absolute freedom or sovereignty of the human will. Men will argue that the will possesses a *self-determining* power. For example, they say, I can turn my eyes up or down; the mind is quite indifferent which I do; the will must decide. But this is a contradiction in terms. This case supposes that I choose one thing in preference to another, while I am in a state of complete indifference. Manifestly, both cannot be true. But it may be replied that the mind was quite indifferent until it came to have a preference. Exactly; and at that time the will was quiescent, too! But the moment indifference vanished, choice was made, and the fact that indifference gave place to preference, overthrows the argument that the will is capable of choosing between two equal things. As we have said, choice implies the acceptance of one alternative and the rejection of the other or others.

That which determines the will is that which causes it to choose. If the will is determined, then there must be a determiner. *What is it* that determines the will? We reply, The strongest motive power which is brought to bear upon it. What this motive power is, varies in different cases. With one it may be the logic of reason, with another the voice of conscience, with another the impulse of the emotions, with another the whisper of the tempter, with another the power of the Holy Spirit; whichever of these presents the *strongest* motive power and exerts the *greatest* influence *upon the individual himself,* is that which impels the will to act. In other words, the action of the will is determined by that condition of mind (which in turn is influenced by the world, the flesh, and the Devil, as well as by God), which has the greatest degree of tendency to excite volition. To illustrate what we have just said, let us analyse a simple example—

On a certain Lord's day afternoon a friend of ours was suffering from a severe headache. He was anxious to visit the sick, but feared that if he did so his own condition would grow worse, and as a consequence, he would be unable to attend the preaching of the Gospel that evening. Two alternatives confronted him: to visit the sick that afternoon and risk being sick himself, or, to take a rest that afternoon (and visit the sick the next day), and probably arise refreshed and fit for the evening service. Now what was it that decided our friend in choosing between these two alternatives? The *will*? Not at all. True, that in the end, the will made a choice, but the will itself was *moved* to make the choice. In the above case certain considerations presented strong motives for selecting either alternative; these motives were balanced the one against the other *by the individual himself*, i.e., his heart and mind, and the one alternative being supported by stronger motives than the other, decision was formed accordingly, *and then* the will acted. On the one side, our friend felt impelled by a sense of duty to visit the sick; he was moved with compassion to do so, and thus a strong motive was presented to his mind. On the other hand, his judgment reminded him that he was feeling far from well himself, that he badly needed a rest, that if he visited the sick his own condition would probably be made worse, and in such case he would be prevented from attending the preaching of the Gospel that night. Furthermore, he knew that on the morrow, the Lord willing, he could visit the sick, and this being so, he concluded he ought to rest that afternoon. Here then were two sets of alternatives presented to our Christian brother: on the one side was a sense of duty plus his own sympathy, on the other side was a sense of his own need plus a real concern for God's glory, for he felt that he *ought* to attend the preaching of the Gospel that night. The latter prevailed. Spiritual considerations outweighed his sense of duty. His decision being taken, the will acted accordingly, and he retired to rest. An analysis of the above case shows that the mind or reasoning faculty was directed by spiritual considerations, and the mind regulated and controlled the will. Hence we say that, if the will is *controlled*, it is neither sovereign nor free, but is the servant of the mind.

It is often taught that the will governs the man, but the Word of God teaches that it is the *heart* which is the dominating centre of our being. Many scriptures might be quoted in substantiation of this. " Keep thy heart with all diligence; for *out of it* are the issues of life " (Prov. 4: 23). " For from within, *out of the heart of men, proceed* evil thoughts, adulteries, fornications, murders," etc. (Mark 7: 21). Here our Lord traces these sinful acts back to their sources, and declares that their fountain is the "heart," and not the will! Again; " This people honoureth Me with their lips, but *their heart* is far from Me " (Matt. 15: 8). If further proof were required we might call attention to the fact that the word " heart " is found in the Bible more than three times as often as the word " will," even though nearly half of the references to the latter refer to *God's* will!

When we affirm that it is the *heart* and not the will which governs the man, we are not merely striving about words, but insisting on a distinction that is of vital importance. Here is an individual before whom two alternatives are placed; which will he choose? We answer, the one which is more agreeable to himself, i.e., his " heart "—the innermost core of his being. Before the sinner is set a life of virtue and piety, and a life of sinful indulgence; which will he follow? The latter. Why? Because this is his choice. But does that prove the will is sovereign? Not at all. Go back from effect to cause. *Why* does the sinner choose a life of sinful indulgence? Because he *prefers* it—and he *does* prefer it, all arguments to the contrary notwithstanding, though of course he does not enjoy the *effects* of such a course. And why does he prefer it? Because his *heart* is sinful. The same alternatives, in like manner, confront the Christian, and he chooses and strives after a life of piety and virtue. Why? Because God has given him a *new heart* or nature. Hence we say it is not the will which makes the sinner impervious to all appeals to " forsake his way," but his corrupt and evil *heart*. He will not come to Christ, *because* he does not want to, and he does not want to because his *heart* hates Him and loves sin: see Jer. 17:9![1]

2. THE BONDAGE OF THE HUMAN WILL.

In any treatise that proposes to deal with the human will, its nature and functions, respect should be had to the will in three different men, namely, unfallen Adam, the sinner, and the Lord Jesus Christ. In unfallen Adam the will was *free*, free in *both* directions, free toward good and free toward evil. But with the sinner it is far otherwise. The sinner is born with a will that is not in a condition of moral equipoise, because in him there is a heart that is "deceitful above all things and desperately wicked," and this gives him *a bias toward evil*. So, too, with the Lord Jesus it was far otherwise: He also differed radically from unfallen Adam. The Lord Jesus Christ *could not sin* because He was "the Holy One of God." Before He was born into this world it was said to Mary, "The Holy Spirit shall come upon thee, and the power of the Highest shall overshadow thee: therefore also *that Holy Thing* which shall be born of thee shall be called

---

[1] It may be asked why, if this is the true condition of man, do the Scriptures address themselves to man's will? Is it not written, "And whosoever *will*, let him take of the water of life freely" (Rev. 22:17)? This fact is readily acknowledged. Such exhortations show that man is responsible to repent, believe and receive Christ, and all these duties involve a response of the will, but, as other Scriptures show, whether or not men do thus respond depends on the state of the nature of which the will is the expression. The will is the *immediate* cause of man's actions, not the *primary* cause.

It is often assumed that man cannot be held responsible for his response to the Gospel unless he is *capable* of choosing Christ; thus it is generally taken for granted that "freewill" and human responsibility are synonymous and that you cannot deny one without denying the other. On the basis of this confusion the Reformed Faith is frequently charged with not doing justice to man's responsibility because it denies his "freewill." (Cf. further note on p. 108.)

The Biblical and Reformed view of man's responsibility is in fact much more profound than the popular Arminian conception. Man is responsible not merely for his will, but for *his whole nature*, and as long as his nature remains what sin (not God) has made it, he "receiveth not the things of the Spirit of God" (1 Cor. 2:14) and he "will not come" to Christ that he might have life (John 5:40). Consequently, while it is every man's duty to receive Christ, it is only the will of a man renewed in his nature by the Holy Spirit that responds to the Gospel.—The Publishers.

the Son of God " (Luke 1 : 35).   Speaking reverently then, we say, that the will of the Son of Man was *not* in a condition of moral equipoise, that is, capable of turning towards either good or evil.   The will of the Lord Jesus was *biased toward that which is good* because, side by side with His sinless, holy, perfect humanity, was His eternal Deity.   Now in contradistinction from the will of the Lord Jesus which was biased toward good, and Adam's will which, before his fall, was in a condition of moral equipoise—capable of turning towards either good or evil—the *sinner's* will is *biased towards evil,* and therefore is " free " in one direction only, namely, in the direction of evil.   The sinner's will is *enslaved* because, as we have already said, it is in bondage to a depraved heart.

In what does the sinner's freedom consist?   This question is naturally suggested by what we have just said above.   The sinner is free in the sense of being unforced *from without*.[1] The sinner is never *forced* to sin.   But the sinner is not free to do *either* good or evil, because an evil heart within is ever inclining him toward sin.   Let us illustrate what we have in mind.   I hold in my hand a book.   I release it; what happens? It falls.   In which direction?   Downwards; always downwards. Why?   Because, answering the law of gravity, its own weight sinks it.   Suppose I desire the book to occupy a position three feet higher, then what?   I must lift it; a power outside of the book must raise it.   Such is the relationship which fallen man

---

[1] It should be clearly remembered that Reformed Theology does not, as is sometimes supposed, deny man's "free agency." Free agency is a separate question from "freewill" (as the latter term is generally used) and the two should not be confused. Cf. *Systematic Theology,* Louis Berkhof, p. 248, and *Systematic Theology,* Charles Hodge, Vol. II, pp. 260, 261. Hodge writes: "The doctrine of man's inability does not assume that man has ceased to be a free moral agent. He is free because he determines his own acts. Every volition is an act of free self-determination. He is a moral agent because he has the consciousness of moral obligation, and whenever he sins he acts freely against the convictions of conscience or the precepts of the moral law. That a man is in such a state that he uniformly prefers and chooses evil instead of good, as do the fallen angels, is no more inconsistent with his free moral agency than his being in such a state as that he prefers and chooses good with the same uniformity that the holy angels do."—The Publishers.

sustains toward God. While Divine power upholds him, he is preserved from plunging still deeper into sin; let the power be withdrawn, and he falls—his own weight (of sin) drags him down. God does not push him down, any more than I did the book. Let all Divine restraint be removed, and every man is capable of becoming, would become, a Cain, a Pharaoh, a Judas. How then is the sinner to move heavenwards? By an act of his own will? Not so. A power outside of himself must grasp hold of him and lift him every inch of the way. The sinner *is* free, but free in one direction only—free to fall, free to sin. As the Word expresses it: "For when ye were the servants of sin, ye were *free from* righteousness" (Rom. 6: 20). The sinner is free to do as he pleases, always as he pleases (except as he is restrained by God), but his pleasure is to sin.

In the opening section of this chapter we insisted that a proper conception of the nature and function of the will is of practical importance, nay, that it constitutes a fundamental test of theological orthodoxy or doctrinal soundness. We wish to amplify this statement and attempt to demonstrate its accuracy. The freedom or bondage of the will was the dividing line between Augustinianism and Pelagianism, and in more recent times between Calvinism and Arminianism. Reduced to simple terms, this means, that the difference involved was the affirmation or denial of the total depravity of man. In making the affirmation we shall now consider,

3. THE IMPOTENCY OF THE HUMAN WILL.

Does it lie within the power of man's will to accept or reject the Lord Jesus Christ as Saviour? Granted that the Gospel is preached to the sinner, that the Holy Spirit convicts him of his lost condition, does it, in the final analysis, lie within the power of his own will to yield himself up to God? Our answer to this question defines our conception of human depravity. That man is a fallen creature all professing Christians will allow, but what many of them mean by "fallen" is often difficult to determine. The general

impression seems to be that man is now mortal, that he is
no longer in the condition in which he left the hands of his
Creator, that he is liable to disease, that he inherits evil ten-
dencies; but, that if he employs his powers to the best of his
ability, somehow he will be happy at last. O, how far short
of the sad truth! Infirmities, sickness, even corporeal death,
are but trifles in comparison with the moral and spiritual
effects of the Fall! It is only by consulting the Holy Scriptures that we are able to obtain some conception of the extent of that terrible calamity.

When we say that man is totally depraved, we mean that
the entrance of sin into the human constitution has affected
every part and faculty of man's being. Total depravity
means that man is, in spirit and soul and body, the slave of
sin and the captive of the Devil—walking " according to the
prince of the power of the air, the spirit that now worketh
in the children of disobedience " (Eph. 2: 2). This statement
ought not to need arguing: it is a common fact of human experience. Man is *unable* to realize his own aspirations and
materialize his own ideals. He *cannot* do the things that he
would. There is a moral inability which paralyses him. This
is proof positive that he is no free man, but instead, the slave
of sin and Satan. " Ye are of your father the Devil, and the
lusts (desires) of your father ye will do " (John 8: 44). Sin
is more than an act or a series of acts; it is a state or condition: it is that which lies behind and produces the acts.
Sin has penetrated and permeated the whole of man's being.
It has blinded the understanding, corrupted the heart,
and alienated the mind from God. *And the will has not
escaped.* The will is under the dominion of sin and Satan.
Therefore, the will is not free. In short, the affections lowe
as they do and the will chooses as it does because of the state
of *the heart,* and because the heart is deceitful above all
things and desperately wicked. " There is *none* that *seeketh*
after God " (Rom. 3: 11).

We repeat our question: Does it lie within the power of the
sinner's wil to yield himself up to God? Let us attempt an
answer by asking several other questions: Can water (of itself)

rise above its own level? Can a clean thing come out of an unclean? Can the will reverse the whole tendency and strain of human nature? Can that which is under the dominion of sin originate that which is pure and holy? Manifestly not. If ever the will of a fallen and depraved creature is to move Godwards, a Divine power must be brought to bear upon it which will overcome the influences of sin that pull in a counter-direction. This is only another way of saying, " No man can come to Me, except the Father which hath sent Me *draw him* " (John 6: 44). In other words, God's people must be *made willing* in the day of His power (Ps. 110: 3). As Mr. J. N. Darby said, " If Christ came to save that which is *lost,* free will has no place. Not that God prevents men from receiving Christ—far from it. But even when God uses all possible inducements, all that is capable of exerting influence in the heart of man, it only serves to show that man will have none of it; that so corrupt is his heart, and so decided his will not to submit to God (however much it may be the devil who encourages him to sin) that nothing can induce him to receive the Lord, and to give up sin. If by the words, ' freedom of man,' they mean that no one forces him to reject the Lord, this liberty fully exists. But if it is said that, on account of the dominion of sin, of which he is the slave, and that voluntarily, he cannot escape from his condition, and make choice of the good—*then he has no liberty whatever* " (italics ours).

The will is not sovereign; it is a servant, because influenced and controlled by the other faculties of man's being. The will is not free because *the man* is the slave of sin— this was clearly implied in our Lord's words, " If the Son therefore shall *make you free,* ye shall be free indeed " (John 8: 36). Man is a rational being and as such responsible and accountable to God, but to affirm that he is capable of choosing that which is spiritually good *is to deny that he is totally depraved*—i.e., depraved in will as in everything else. Because man's will is governed by his mind and heart, and because these have been vitiated and corrupted by sin, then it follows that if ever man is to turn or move in a Godward direction, God Himself must work in him " both *to will and to do* of His good pleasure " (Phil. 2 : 13).   Man's boasted freedom is, in truth, " the bondage of corruption "; he " *serves* divers lusts and pleasures."   Said a deeply-taught servant of God, " Man is impotent as to his will.   He has no will favourable to God.   I believe in free will; but then it is a *will only free to act according to its nature* (italics ours).   A dove has no will to eat carrion; a raven has no will to eat the clean food of the dove.   Put the nature of the dove into the raven and it will eat the food of the dove.   Satan could have no will for holiness.   We speak it with reverence, God could have no will for evil.   The sinner in his sinful nature could never have a will according to God.   For this he must be born again " (J. Denham Smith).   This is precisely what we have contended for throughout this chapter—*the will is regulated by the nature.*

Among the " decrees " of the Council of Trent (1563), which is the avowed standard of Popery, we find the following (in the Canons on Justification):

" If any one shall affirm, that man's free-will, moved and excited by God, does not, by consenting, co-operate with God, the mover and exciter, so as to *dispose* and *prepare* itself for the *attainment* of justification; if moreover, anyone shall say, that the human will cannot refuse complying, if *it pleases*; but that it is unactive, and merely passive; let such an one *be accursed* " !

" If anyone shall affirm, that since the fall of Adam, man's free-will *is lost* and extinguished; or, that it is a thing titular, yea a name, without a thing, and a fiction introduced by Satan into the Church; let such an one *be accursed* " !

Thus, those who today insist on the free-will of the natural man believe precisely what Rome teaches on the subject !

In order for any sinner to be saved three things were indispensable: God the Father had to *purpose* his salvation, God the Son had to *purchase* it, God the Spirit has to *apply* it.   God does more than " propose " to us.   Were He *only* to " invite," every one of us would be lost.   This is strikingly illustrated in the Old Testament.   In Ezra 1 : 1-3 we read,

" Now in the first year of Cyrus king of Persia, that the word of the Lord by the mouth of Jeremiah might be fulfilled, the Lord stirred up the spirit of Cyrus king of Persia, that he made a proclamation throughout all his kingdom, and put it also in writing, saying, Thus saith Cyrus king of Persia, The Lord God of heaven hath given me all the kingdoms of the earth; and He hath charged me to build Him an house at Jerusalem, which is in Judah. Who is there among you of all His people? his God be with him, and let him go up to Jerusalem, which is in Judah, and build the house of the Lord God of Israel."   Here was an " offer " made, made to a people in captivity, affording them opportunity to leave and return to Jerusalem—God's dwelling-place. Did *all* Israel eagerly respond to this offer? No indeed! The vast majority were content to remain in the enemy's land.   Only a " remnant " availed themselves of this overture of mercy! And *why* did *they*? Hear the answer of Scripture: " Then rose up the chief of the fathers of Judah and Benjamin, and the priests, and the Levites, with all whose spirit *God had stirred up*, to go up to build the house of the Lord which is in Jerusalem " (Ezra 1 : 5)!   In like manner, *God* " stirs up " the spirits of His elect when the effectual call comes to them, and not till then do they have any *willingness to* respond to the Divine proclamation.

The superficial work of many of the professional evangelists of the last fifty years is largely responsible for the erroneous views now current upon the *bondage* of the natural man, encouraged by the laziness of those in the pew in their failure to " *prove* all things " (1 Thess. 5 : 21).   The average evangelical pulpit conveys the impression that it lies wholly in the power of the sinner whether or not he shall be saved. It is said that " God has done His part, now man must do his." Alas, what *can* a lifeless man do, and man by nature is " *dead* in trespasses and sins " (Eph. 2 : 1)!   If the truth were really believed, there would be more dependence upon the Holy Spirit to come in with His miracle-working power, and less confidence in *our* attempts to " win men for Christ."

When addressing the unsaved, preachers often draw an

analogy between God's sending of the Gospel to the sinner, and a sick man in bed, with healing medicine on a table by his side: all he needs to do is to reach forth his hand and take it.   But in order for this illustration to be in any wise true to the picture which Scripture gives us of the fallen and depraved sinner, the sick man in bed must be described as one who is blind (Eph. 4: 18) so that he cannot see the medicine, his hand paralysed (Rom. 5: 6) so that he is unable to reach forth for it, and his heart not only devoid of all confidence in the medicine but filled with hatred against the physician himself (John 15: 18). O what superficial views of man's desperate plight are now entertained!   Christ came here not to help those who were willing to help themselves, but to do for His people what they were incapable of doing for themselves: " To open the blind eyes, to bring out the prisoners from the prison, and them that sit in darkness out of the prison house " (Isa. 42: 7).

Now, in conclusion, let us anticipate and dispose of the usual and inevitable objection—*Why preach the Gospel if man is powerless to respond?* Why bid the sinner come to Christ if sin has so enslaved him that he has no power in himself *to* come?   We reply: —We do not preach the Gospel because we believe that man has a " free-will " and is therefore able to receive Christ, but we preach it *because we are commanded to do so*[1] (Mark 16: 15); and though to them that perish it is *foolishness,* yet, " unto us which are saved it is *the power of God*" (1 Cor. 1: 18).   " The foolishness of God is wiser than men; and the weakness of God is stronger than men " (1 Cor. 1: 25).   The sinner is dead in trespasses and sins (Eph. 2: 1), and a dead man is utterly incapable of willing anything; hence it is that " they that are in the flesh (the unregenerate) cannot please God " (Rom. 8: 8).

To fleshly wisdom it appears the height of folly to preach the Gospel to those that are *dead,* and therefore *beyond* the

---

[1] Cf. *Historical Theology*, William Cunningham, Vol II, pp. 347-8: "The sole ground or warrant for men's act, in offering pardon and salvation to their fellow-men, is the authority and command of God in His word."—The Publishers.

reach of doing anything themselves. Yes, but God's ways are different from ours. It pleases God " by the *foolishness of preaching* to save them that believe " (1 Cor. 1:21). Man may deem it folly to prophesy to "*dead bones*" and to say unto them, " O, ye dry bones, hear the Word of the Lord " (Ezek. 37:4). Ah! but then it is the Word *of the Lord*, and the words He speaks "they are spirit, *and they are life*" (John 6:63). Wise men standing by the grave of Lazarus might pronounce it an evidence of insanity when the Lord addressed a *dead* man with the words, " Lazarus, come forth." Ah! but He who thus spake was and is Himself the Resurrection and the Life, and at *His* word even the dead live! We go forth to preach the Gospel, then, not because we believe that sinners have within themselves the power to receive the Saviour it proclaims, but because the Gospel itself *is the power of God unto* salvation to everyone that believeth, and because we know that " as many as were ordained to eternal life " (Acts 13:48), *shall* believe (John 6:37; 10:16 —note the " shall's "!) in God's appointed time, for it is written, " Thy people *shall* be willing in the day of *Thy* power " (Ps. 110:3)!

What we have set forth in this chapter is not a product of "modern thought"; no indeed, it is at direct variance with it. Men of the past few generations have *departed* far from the teachings of their scripturally-instructed fathers. In the thirty-nine Articles of the Church of England we read, " The condition of man after the fall of Adam is such, that he cannot turn and prepare himself, by his own natural strength and good works, to faith, and calling upon God: Wherefore we have *no power* to do good works pleasant and acceptable to God, without the grace of God by Christ preventing us (being before-hand with us), that we may have a good will, and working with us, when we have that good will " (Article 10). In the Westminster Larger Catechism (which used to be recognized by all Presbyterian Churches) we read, " The sinfulness of that state whereinto man fell, consisteth in the guilt of Adam's first sin, the want of that righteousness wherein he was created, and the corruption of his nature, whereby he is utterly indisposed, disabled, and made opposite unto all that is spiritually good, and wholly inclined to all evil, and that continually " (Answer to question 25). So in the Baptists' Philadelphian Confession of Faith (1742), we read, " Man, by his fall into a state of sin, hath wholly lost *all ability of will* to any spiritual good accompanying salvation; so as a natural man, being altogether averse from good, and dead in sin, is not able by his own strength to convert himself, or to prepare himself thereunto " (Chapter 9).

Note on Responsibility.

The assumption that responsibility implies ability is a philosophical argument and not a biblical one. It was nevertheless popularized in the last century by such evangelists as C. G. Finney and has become almost universally accepted. Reviewing Finney's position, Charles Hodge wrote:

" With him it is a ' first truth ' that freedom of the will is essential to moral obligation, and that no man is bound to do what is not in his own power.

" The fallacy of which he is guilty is very obvious. He transfers a maxim which is an axiom in one department, to another in which it has no legitimate force. It is a first truth that a man without eyes cannot be under an obligation to see, or a man without ears to hear. Within the sphere therefore of physical impossibilities, the maxim that obligation is limited by ability, is undoubtedly true. But it is no less obviously true that an inability which has its origin in sin, which consists in what is sinful, and relates to moral action, is perfectly consistent with continued obligation. It is one of the most familiar facts of consciousness, that a sense of obligation is consistent with a conviction of entire inability. It is a dictum of philosophers, ' I ought, therefore, I can.' To which every heart burdened with a sense of sin replies, ' I ought to be able, but I am not.' Such is the testimony of conscience and such is the plain doctrine of the Bible. . . . It was, says Neander, the radical principle of Pelagius' system that he assumed moral liberty to consist in the ability to choose between good and evil."—Charles Hodge, *Essay and Reviews*, pp. 252-261.

GOD'S SOVEREIGNTY AND PRAYER

" If we ask anything according to *His* will, He heareth us "
(1 JOHN 5:14).

THROUGHOUT this book it has been our chief aim to
exalt the Creator and abase the creature. The well-nigh
universal tendency, now, is to magnify man and dishonour
and degrade God. On every hand it will be found that, when
spiritual things are under discussion, the human side and
element is pressed and stressed, and the Divine side, if not
altogether ignored, is relegated to the background. This
holds true of very much of the modern teaching about prayer.
In the great majority of the books written, and in the sermons preached upon prayer, the human element fills the
scene almost entirely: it is the conditions which *we* must
meet, the promises *we* must " claim," the things *we* must do,
in order to get our requests granted; and *God's* claims, *God's*
rights, *God's* glory are often disregarded.

As a fair sample of what is being given out today we sub-
join a brief editorial (entitled " Prayer, or Fate?"), which
appeared recently in one of the leading religious weeklies.

" God in His sovereignty has ordained that human destinies may be changed and moulded by the will of man.
This is at the heart of the truth that prayer changes
things, meaning that God changes things when men pray.
Someone has strikingly expressed it this way: 'There are
certain things that will happen in a man's life whether he
prays or not. There are other things that will happen if
he prays, and will not happen if he does not pray.' A
Christian worker was impressed by these sentences as he
entered a business office, and he prayed that the Lord
would open the way to speak to someone about Christ,
reflecting that things would be changed because he prayed.

Then his mind turned to other things and the prayer was forgotten. The opportunity came to speak to the business man on whom he was calling, but he did not grasp it, and was on his way out when he remembered his prayer of a half hour before, and God's answer. He promptly returned and had a talk with the business man, who, though a church-member, had never in his life been asked whether he was saved. Let us give ourselves to prayer, and open the way for God to change things. Let us beware lest we become virtual fatalists by failing to exercise our God-given wills in praying."

The above illustrates what is now being taught on the subject of prayer, and the deplorable thing is that scarcely a voice is lifted in protest. To say that "human destinies *may be changed* and moulded *by the will of man*" is rank infidelity—that is the only proper term for it. Should any one challenge this classification, we would ask them whether they can find an infidel anywhere who would dissent from such a statement, and we are confident that such an one could not be found. To say that "*God* has *ordained* that human destinies may be changed and moulded by the will of man," is absolutely untrue. "Human destiny" is settled *not* by "the will of man," but by the will of God. That which determines human destiny is whether or not a man has been born again, for it is written, "Except a man be born again he cannot see the kingdom of God." And as to *whose* will, whether God's or man's, is responsible for the new birth is settled, unequivocally, by John 1:13—"Which were born, not of blood, nor of the will of the flesh, *nor of the will of man*, but OF GOD." To say that "human destiny" may be *changed* by the will of man, is to make the creature's will *supreme*, and that is, virtually to *dethrone* God. But what saith the Scriptures? Let the Book answer: "The Lord killeth, and maketh alive: *He* bringeth down to the grave, and bringeth up. The Lord maketh poor, and maketh rich: *He* bringeth low, and lifteth up. *He* raiseth up the poor out of the dust, and lifteth up the beggar from the dunghill, to set them among princes, and to make them inherit the throne of glory" (1 Sam. 2 : 6-8).

Turning back to the editorial here under review, we are next told, "This is at the heart of the truth that prayer changes things, meaning that God changes things when men pray." Almost everywhere we go today, we come across a motto-card bearing the inscription "Prayer Changes Things." What these words are designed to signify is evident from the current literature on prayer—*we* are to persuade God to *change* His purpose. Concerning this we shall have more to say below.

Again, the Editor tells us, "Some one has strikingly expressed it this way: 'There are certain things that will happen in a man's life whether he prays or not. There are other things that will happen if he prays, and will not happen if he does not pray.'" That things happen whether a man prays or not is exemplified daily in the lives of the unregenerate, most of whom never pray at all. That "other things will happen if he prays" is in need of qualification. If a believer prays in faith and asks for those things which are according to God's will, he will most certainly obtain that for which he has asked. Again, that other things will happen if he prays, is also true in respect to the subjective benefits derived from prayer: God will become more real to him and His promises more precious. That other things "will not happen if he does not pray" is true so far as his own life is concerned —a prayerless life means a life lived out of communion with God and all that is involved by this. But to affirm that God will not and cannot bring to pass His eternal purpose unless we pray, is utterly erroneous, for the same God who has decreed the end has also decreed that His end shall be reached through His appointed means, and one of these is prayer. The God who has determined to grant a blessing, also gives a spirit of supplication which first seeks the blessing.

The example (of the Christian worker and the business man) cited in the above editorial, is a very unhappy one. According to the terms of the illustration, the Christian worker's prayer was not answered by God at all, inasmuch as, apparently, the way was not opened to speak to the business man about his soul.   But on leaving the office and recalling his prayer, the Christian worker (perhaps in the energy of the flesh) determined to answer the prayer *for himself,* and instead of leaving the Lord to " open the way " for him, took matters into his own hand.

We quote next from one of the latest books issued on Prayer.   In it the author says, " The possibilities and necessity of prayer, its power and results, are manifested in arresting and *changing the purposes of God* and in relieving the stroke of His power."   Such an assertion as this is a horrible reflection upon the character of the Most High God, who " doeth according to His will in the army of heaven, and among the inhabitants of the earth: and *none can stay His hand,* or say unto Him, What doest Thou?" (Dan. 4: 35). There is *no need* whatever *for* God to change His designs or alter His purpose, for the all-sufficient reason that these were framed under the influence of perfect goodness and unerring wisdom.   *Men* may have occasion to alter *their* purposes, for in their short-sightedness they are frequently unable to anticipate what may arise *after* their plans are formed.   But not so with God, for He knows the end from the beginning.   To affirm that God changes His purpose is either to impugn His goodness or to deny His eternal wisdom.

In the same book we are told, " The prayers of God's saints are the capital stock in heaven by which Christ carries on His great work upon earth.   The great throes and mighty convulsions on earth are the results of these prayers.   Earth is changed, revolutionized, angels move on more powerful, more rapid wing, and *God's policy is shaped* as the prayers are more numerous, more efficient."   If possible, this is even worse, and we have no hesitation in declaring it to be written in defiance of the teaching of Scripture.   In the first place, it flatly denies Eph. 3: 11, which speaks of God's having an " *eternal* purpose."   If God's purpose is an eternal one, then His " policy " is *not* being " shaped " today.   In the second place, it contradicts Eph. 1: 11 which expressly declares that God " worketh *all* things after the counsel of *His own* will ";

therefore it follows that "God's policy" is *not* being
"shaped" by man's prayers. In the third place, such a statement as the above makes the will of the creature supreme, for
if *our* prayers shape *God's* policy, then is the Most High subordinate to worms of the earth. Well might the Holy Spirit
ask through the apostle, "For who hath known the mind of
the Lord? *or who hath been His counsellor*?" (Rom. 11: 34).

Such thoughts on prayer as we have been citing are due to
low and inadequate conceptions of God Himself. It ought
to be apparent that there could be little or no comfort in
praying to a God who was like the chameleon, which changes
its colour every day. What encouragement is there to lift up
our hearts to One who was in one mind yesterday and is in
another today? What would be the use of petitioning an
earthly monarch, if we knew he was so mutable as to grant
a petition one day and deny it another? Is it not the very
unchangeableness of God which is our greatest encouragement *to pray*? Because He is "*without* variableness or
shadow of turning" we are assured that if we ask anything
according to His will we are most certain of being heard.
Well did Luther remark, "Prayer is not overcoming God's
reluctance, but laying hold of His willingness."

And this leads us to offer a few remarks concerning the
design of prayer. *Why* has God appointed that we should
pray? The vast majority of people would reply, In order
that we may obtain from God the things which we need.
While this *is* one of the purposes of prayer, it is by no means
the chief one. Moreover, it considers prayer only from the
human side, and prayer sadly needs to be viewed from the
Divine side. Let us look, then, at some of the reasons why
God has bidden us to pray.

First and foremost, prayer has been appointed that the
Lord God Himself should be *honoured*. God requires us to
recognize that He is, indeed, "the *high* and *lofty* One that
inhabiteth eternity" (Isa. 57: 17). God requires that we shall
own His *universal dominion*: in petitioning God for rain,
Elijah did but confess His control over the elements; in praying to God to deliver a poor sinner from the wrath to come,

we acknowledge that " salvation is of the Lord " (Jonah 2 : 9); in supplicating His blessing on the Gospel unto the uttermost parts of the earth, we declare His rulership over the whole world.

Again; God requires that we shall *worship* Him and prayer, real prayer, is an act of worship. Prayer is an act of worship inasmuch as it is the prostrating of the soul before Him; inasmuch as it is a calling upon His great and holy name; inasmuch as it is the owning of His goodness, His power, His immutability, His grace; and inasmuch as it is the recognition of His sovereignty, owned by a submission to His will. It is highly significant to notice in this connection that the Temple was not termed by Christ the House of Sacrifice, but instead, the House of Prayer.

Again; prayer *redounds to God's glory,* for in prayer we do but acknowledge our dependency upon Him. When we humbly supplicate the Divine Being we cast ourselves upon His power and mercy. In seeking blessings from God we own that He is the Author and Fountain of every good and perfect gift. That prayer brings glory to God is further seen from the fact that prayer calls faith into exercise, and nothing from us is so honouring and pleasing to Him as the confidence of our hearts.

In the second place, prayer is appointed by God *for our spiritual blessing,* as a means for *our growth in grace.* When we seek to learn the *design* of prayer, this should ever occupy us *before* we regard prayer as a means for obtaining the supply of our need. Prayer is designed by God for our *humbling.* Prayer, real prayer, is a coming into the Presence of God, and a sense of His awful majesty produces a realization of our nothingness and unworthiness. Again; prayer is designed by God for *the exercise of our faith.* Faith is begotten in the Word (Rom. 10: 17), but it is exercised in prayer; hence, we read of " the prayer of faith." Again; prayer calls *love* into action. Concerning the hypocrite the question is asked, " Will he delight himself in the Almighty? Will he always call upon God?" (Job 27: 10). But they that love the Lord cannot be long away from Him, for they *delight* in unburdening themselves to him. Not only does prayer call love into action, but through the direct answers vouchsafed to our prayers, our love to God is increased—" I love the Lord, *because* He hath heard my voice and my supplications" (Ps. 116: 1). Again; prayer is designed by God to teach us the *value* of the blessings we have sought from Him, and it causes us to rejoice the more when He *has* bestowed upon us that for which we supplicate Him.

Third, prayer is appointed by God for our seeking from Him the things which we are in need of. But here a difficulty may present itself to those who have read carefully the previous chapters of this book. If God has fore-ordained, before the foundation of the world, everything which happens in time, what is the use of prayer? If it is true that " of Him and through Him and to Him are *all things* " (Rom. 11: 36), then why pray? Ere we reply directly to these queries it should be pointed out that there is just as much reason to ask, What is the use of my coming to God and telling Him what He already knows? wherein is the use of my spreading before Him my need, seeing He is already acquainted with it? as there is to object, What is the use of praying for anything when everything has been ordained beforehand by God? Prayer is not for the purpose of informing God, as if He were ignorant (the Saviour expressly declared " for your Father knoweth what things ye have need of, before ye ask Him "—Matt. 6: 8), but it is to acknowledge He *does* know what we are in need of. Prayer is not appointed for the furnishing of God with the knowledge of what we need, but it is designed as a confession to Him of *our sense* of the need. In this, as in everything, God's thoughts are not as ours. God requires that His gifts should be sought for. He designs to be *honoured* by our asking, just as He is to be *thanked* by us after He has bestowed His blessing.

However, the question still returns on us, If God has predestined everything that comes to pass, and if He regulates all events, then is not prayer a profitless exercise? A sufficient answer to these questions is, that God *bids* us to pray—" *Pray* without ceasing " (1 Thess. 5: 17). And again, " men *ought*

always to pray" (Luke 18: 1). And further: Scripture declares that, " the prayer of faith shall save the sick," and, " the
effectual fervent prayer of a righteous man availeth much "
(Jas. 5: 15, 16); while the Lord Jesus Christ—our perfect Example in all things—was pre-eminently a Man of Prayer.
Thus it is evident that prayer is neither meaningless nor
valueless. But still this does not *remove* the difficulty nor
answer the question with which we started out. What then
is the *relationship* between God's sovereignty and Christian
prayer?

First of all, we would say with emphasis, that prayer is
not intended to *change* God's purpose, nor is it to move Him
to form fresh purposes. God has decreed that certain events
shall come to pass, but He has also decreed that these events
shall come to pass through the means He has appointed for
their accomplishment. God has elected certain ones to be
saved, but He has also decreed that they shall be saved
through the preaching of the Gospel. The Gospel, then, is
one of the appointed means for the working out of the eternal counsel of the Lord; and prayer is another. God has decreed the means as well as the end, and among the means is
prayer. Even the prayers of His people are included in His
eternal decrees. Therefore, instead of prayers being in vain,
they are among the means through which God fulfils His decrees. " If indeed all things happen by a blind chance, or
a fatal necessity, prayers in that case could be of no moral
efficacy, and of no use; but since they are regulated by the
direction of Divine wisdom, prayers have a place in the order
of events " (Haldane).

That prayers for the execution of the very things *decreed*
by God are *not* meaningless, is clearly taught in the Scriptures. Elijah *knew* that God *was* about to give rain, but
that did not prevent him from at once betaking himself to
prayer (Jas. 5: 17, 18). Daniel " understood " by the writings
of the prophets that the captivity was to last but seventy
years, yet when these seventy years were almost ended, we are
told that he " set his face unto the Lord God, *to seek* by
prayer and supplications, with fasting and sackcloth and

ashes" (Dan. 9: 2, 3). God told the prophet Jeremiah, "For
I know the thoughts that I think toward you, saith the Lord,
thoughts of peace, and not of evil, to give you an expected
end"; but instead of adding, there is, therefore, no need for
you to supplicate Me for these things, He said, "*Then* shall
ye call upon Me, and ye shall go and pray unto Me, and I
will hearken unto you" (Jer. 29: 11-12).

Once more; in Ezek. 36 we read of the explicit, positive,
and unconditional promises which God has made concerning the future restoration of Israel, yet in verse 37 of this
same chapter we are told, "Thus saith the Lord God; *I will
yet for this be enquired of* by the house of Israel, to do it for
them"! Here then is *the* design of prayer: not that God's
will may be *altered*, but that it may be *accomplished* in His
own good time and way. It is because God *has* promised certain things, that we can ask for them with the full assurance
of faith. It is God's purpose that His will shall be brought
about by His own appointed means, and that He may do His
people good upon *His own* terms, and that is, by the
"means" and "terms" of entreaty and supplication. Did
not the Son of God *know* for certain that after His death and
resurrection He *would be* exalted by the Father? Assuredly
He did. Yet we find Him *asking for* this very thing: "Now,
O Father, glorify Thou Me with Thine Own Self with the
glory which I had with Thee before the world was" (John
17: 5)! Did not He know that none of His people could
perish? yet He besought the Father to "keep" them (John
17: 11)!

Finally; it should be said that God's will is immutable, and
cannot be altered by our cryings. When the mind of God is
not toward a people to do them good, it cannot be turned to
them by the most fervent and importunate prayers of those
who have the greatest interest in Him—"Then said the Lord
unto me, Though Moses and Samuel stood before Me, *yet My
mind could not be* toward this people: cast them out of My
sight, and let them go forth" (Jer. 15: 1). The prayers of
Moses to enter the promised land is a parallel case.

Our views respecting prayer need to be revised and

brought into harmony with the teaching of Scripture on the subject. The prevailing idea seems to be, that I come to God and *ask* Him for something that I want, and that I *expect* Him to give me that which I have asked. But this is a most dishonouring and degrading conception. The popular belief reduces God to a servant, *our* servant: doing our bidding, performing our pleasure, granting our desires. No; prayer is a coming to God, telling Him my *need*, committing my way unto the Lord, and leaving Him to deal with it as seemeth *Him* best. *This* makes my will subject to His, instead of, as in the former case, seeking to bring His will into subjection to mine. No prayer is pleasing to God unless the spirit actuating it is, "*not* my will, but thine be done." "When God bestows blessings on a praying people, it is not for the sake of their prayers, as if He was inclined and turned by them; but it is for His own sake, and of His own sovereign will and pleasure. Should it be said, To what purpose then is prayer? it is answered, This is the way and means God has appointed, for the communication of the blessings of His goodness to His people. For though He has purposed, provided, and promised them, yet He will be sought unto, to give them, and it is a duty and privilege to ask. When they are blessed with a spirit of prayer, it forebodes well, and looks as if God intended to bestow the good things asked, which should be asked always with submission to the will of God, saying, *Not my will but Thine be done*" (John Gill).

The distinction just noted is of great practical importance for our peace of heart. Perhaps the one thing that exercises Christians as much as anything else is that of *un*-answered prayers. They have asked God for something: so far as they are able to judge, they have asked in faith, believing they would receive that for which they have supplicated the Lord: and they have asked earnestly and repeatedly, *but* the answer has not come. The result is that, in many cases, faith in the efficacy of prayer becomes weakened, until hope gives way to despair and the throne of grace is altogether neglected. Is it not so?

Now will it surprise our readers when we say that *every*

real prayer of faith that has ever been offered to God *has been* answered? Yet we unhesitatingly affirm it. But in saying this we must refer back to our definition of prayer. Let us repeat it. Prayer is a coming to God, telling Him our *need* (or the need or others), committing our way unto the Lord, and then leaving Him to deal with the case as seemeth Him best. This leaves God to answer the prayer in whatever way He sees fit, and often, His answer may be the very opposite of what would be most acceptable to the flesh; yet, if we have *really LEFT* our need in His hands, it will be His *answer,* nevertheless. Let us look at two examples.

In John 11 we read of the sickness of Lazarus. The Lord "loved" him, but He was absent from Bethany. The sisters sent a messenger unto the Lord to acquaint Him with their brother's condition. And note particularly *how* their appeal was worded—"Lord, behold, he whom Thou lovest is sick." That was all. They did not ask Him to heal Lazarus. They did not request Him to hasten at once to Bethany. They simply spread their need before Him, committed the case into His hands, and left Him to act as *He* deemed best! And what was our Lord's reply? Did He respond to their appeal and answer their mute request? Certainly He did, though not, perhaps, in the way they had hoped. He answered by abiding "two days still in the same place where He was" (John 11:6), and allowing Lazarus to die! But in this instance, that was not all. Later, He journeyed to Bethany and raised Lazarus from the dead. Our purpose in referring here to this case, is to illustrate the proper attitude for the believer to take before God in the hour of need. The next example will emphasize, rather, God's method of responding to His needy child.

Turn to 2 Cor. 12. The apostle Paul has been accorded an unheard-of privilege. He has been transported into Paradise. His ears have listened to and his eyes have gazed upon that which no other mortal has heard or seen this side of death. The wondrous revelation was more than the apostle could endure. He was in danger of becoming "puffed up" by his extraordinary experience. Therefore, a thorn in the

flesh, the messenger of Satan, is sent to buffet him lest he be
exalted above measure. And the apostle spreads his need before the Lord; he thrice beseeches Him that this thorn in
the flesh should be *removed*. Was his prayer answered?
Assuredly, though not in the manner he had desired. The
" thorn " was not removed, but grace was given to bear it.
The burden was not lifted, but strength was vouchsafed to
carry it.

Does someone object that it is our privilege to do more
than spread our need before God? Are we reminded that
God has, as it were, given us a blank cheque and invited us
to fill it in? Is it said that the promises of God are all-in-
clusive, and that we may *ask God for what we will*? If so,
we must call attention to the fact that it is necessary to compare scripture with scripture if we are to learn the full mind
of God on any subject, and that as this is done we discover
God has *qualified* the promises given to praying souls by saying, " If we ask anything *according to His will* He heareth
us" (1 John 5: 14). Real prayer is communion with God, so
that there will be common thoughts between His mind and
ours. What is needed is for Him to fill our hearts with *His*
thoughts, and then His desires will become *our* desires flow-
ing back to Him. Here then is the meeting-place between
God's sovereignty and Christian prayer: If we ask anything
according to *His will* He heareth us, and if we do *not* so ask,
He *does not* hear us; as saith the apostle James, " Ye ask, and
receive not, *because ye ask amiss*, that ye might consume it
upon *your* lusts " or desires (4: 3).

But did not the Lord Jesus tell His disciples, " Verily,
verily, I say unto you, *Whatsoever* ye shall ask the Father
in My name, He will give it you " (John 16: 23)? He did;
but this promise does not give praying souls *carte blanche*.
These words of our Lord are in perfect accord with those of
the apostle John—" If we ask anything according to His will
He heareth us." What is it to ask " in the name of Christ "?
Surely it is very much more than a prayer formula, the mere
concluding of our supplications with the *words*, " in the
name of Christ." To apply to God for anything in the name

of Christ, it must needs be in keeping with what Christ is! To ask God in the name of Christ is as though Christ Himself were the suppliant. *We can only ask God for what Christ would ask*. To ask in the name of Christ, is therefore, to *set aside* our own wills, accepting God's!

Let us now amplify our definition of prayer. What is prayer? Prayer is not so much an act as it is an *attitude*—an attitude of *dependency*, dependency upon God. Prayer is a confession of creature weakness, yea, of helplessness. Prayer is the acknowledgment of our need and the spreading of it before God. We do not say that this is *all* there is in prayer; it is not. But it *is* the essential, the primary element in prayer. We freely admit that we are quite unable to give a *complete* definition of prayer within the compass of a brief sentence, or in any number of words. Prayer is both an attitude *and* an act, a *human* act, and yet there is the Divine element in it too, and it is this which makes an exhaustive analysis impossible as well as impious to attempt. But admitting this, we do insist again, that prayer is fundamentally an attitude of dependency upon God. Therefore, prayer is the very opposite of *dictating* to God. Because prayer is an attitude of dependency, the one who really prays is *submissive*, submissive to the Divine will; and submission to the Divine will means, that we are content for the Lord to supply our need according to the dictates of His own sovereign pleasure. And hence it is that we say, *every prayer* that is offered to God in *this* spirit is sure of meeting with an answer or response from Him.

Here then is the reply to our opening question, and the scriptural solution to the seeming difficulty. Prayer is not the requesting of God to alter His purpose or for Him to form a new one. Prayer is the taking of an attitude of dependency upon God, the spreading of our need before Him, the asking for those things which are in accordance with His will, and therefore there is nothing whatever *inconsistent* between Divine sovereignty and Christian prayer.

In closing this chapter we would utter a word of caution to safeguard the reader against drawing a false conclusion from what has been said. We have not here sought to *epitomize* the whole teaching of Scripture on the subject of prayer, nor have we even attempted to discuss in general the *problem* of prayer; instead, we have confined ourselves, more or less, to a consideration of the *relationship* between God's Sovereignty and Christian Prayer. What we have written is intended chiefly as a protest *against* much of the modern teaching, which so stresses the *human* element in prayer, that the Divine side is almost entirely lost sight of.

In Jer. 10: 23 we are told "It is not in man that walketh to direct his steps" (cf. Prov. 16: 9); and yet in many of his prayers, man impiously presumes to direct the Lord as to *His* way, and as to what *He* ought to do: even implying that if only *he* had the direction of the affairs of the world and of the Church, *he* would soon have things very different from what they are. This cannot be denied: for anyone with any spiritual discernment at all could not fail to detect this spirit in many of our modern prayer-meetings where the flesh holds sway. How slow we all are to learn the lesson that the haughty creature needs to be brought down to his knees and humbled into the dust. *And this is where the very act of prayer is intended to put us.* But man (with his usual perversity) turns the footstool into a throne, from whence he would fain direct the Almighty as to what He *ought* to do! giving the onlooker the impression that if God had half the compassion that those who " pray " have, all would quickly be put right! Such is the arrogance of the old nature even in a child of God.

Our main purpose in this chapter has been to emphasize the need for submitting, in prayer, *our wills to God's*. But it must also be added, that prayer is much more than a pious exercise, and far otherwise than a mechanical performance. Prayer is, indeed, a Divinely-appointed means whereby we may obtain from God the things we ask, *provided* that we ask for those things which are in accord with *His will*. These pages will have been penned in vain unless they lead both writer and reader to cry with a deeper earnestness than heretofore, " Lord, *teach us* to pray " (Luke 11: 1).

OUR ATTITUDE TOWARDS GOD'S SOVEREIGNTY

" Even so, Father: for so it seemed good in Thy sight "
(MATT. 11:26).

IN the present chapter we shall consider, somewhat briefly,
the practical application to ourselves of the great truth
which we have pondered in its various ramifications in earlier
pages. In the next chapter we shall deal more in detail with
the *value* of this doctrine, but here we would confine ourselves to a definition of what ought to be our *attitude toward*
the sovereignty of God.

Every truth that is revealed to us in God's Word is there
not only for our information but also for our inspiration.
The Bible has been given to us not to gratify an idle curios-
ity but to edify our souls. The sovereignty of God is something more than an abstract principle which explains the
rationale of the Divine government: it is designed as a motive for godly fear, it is made known to us for the promotion
of righteous living, it is revealed in order to bring into subjection our rebellious hearts. A true re*cognition* of God's
sovereignty humbles as nothing else does or can humble, and
brings the heart into lowly submission before God, causing
us to relinquish our own self-will and making us delight in
the perception and performance of the Divine will.

When we speak of the sovereignty of God we mean very
much more than the *exercise* of God's governmental power,
though, of course, that is included in the expression. As we
have remarked in an earlier chapter, the sovereignty of God
means the Godhood of God. In its fullest and deepest meaning the title of this book signifies the *Character* and *Being*
of the One whose pleasure is performed and whose will is
executed. Truly to recognize the sovereignty of God is,
therefore, to gaze upon the Sovereign Himself. It is to come

123

into the presence of the august " Majesty on High." It is to have a sight of the thrice-holy God in His excellent glory. The *effects* of such a sight may be learned from those scriptures which describe the experience of different ones who obtained a view of the Lord God.

Mark the experience of Job—the one of whom the Lord Himself said, " There is none like him in the earth, a perfect and an upright man, one that feareth God, and escheweth evil " (Job 1 : 8). At the close of the book which bears his name we are shown Job in the Divine presence, and how does he carry himself when brought face to face with Jehovah? Hear what he says: "I have heard of Thee by the hearing of the ear; but now mine eye seeth Thee: Wherefore *I abhor* myself, and *repent* in dust and ashes " (Job. 42 : 5, 6). Thus, a sight of God, God revealed in awesome majesty, caused Job to abhor himself, and not only so, but to *abase* himself before the Almighty.

Take note of Isaiah. In the sixth chapter of his prophecy a scene is brought before us which has few equals even in Scripture. The prophet beholds the Lord upon the Throne, a Throne " high and lifted up." Above this Throne stood the seraphim with veiled faces, crying, " Holy, holy, holy, is the Lord of hosts." What is the *effect of this sight upon* the prophet? We read, " *Then* said I, Woe is me! for I am undone; because I am a man of unclean lips, and dwell in the midst of a people of unclean lips: for mine eyes have seen the King, the Lord of hosts " (Isa. 6 : 5). A sight of the Divine *King* humbled Isaiah into the dust, bringing him, as it did, to a realization of his own nothingness.

Once more. Look at the prophet Daniel. Towards the close of his life this man of God beheld the Lord in theophanic manifestation. He appeared to His servant in human form, " clothed in linen " and with loins " girded with fine gold "—symbolic of holiness and Divine glory. We read that, " His body also was like the beryl, and His face as the appearance of lightning, and His eyes as lamps of fire, and His arms and His feet like in colour to polished brass, and the voice of His words like the voice of a multitude." Daniel

then tells of the effect this vision had upon him and those
who were with him—" And I Daniel alone saw the vision: for
the men that were with me saw not the vision; but a great
quaking fell upon them, so that they fled to hide themselves.
Therefore I was left alone, and saw this great vision, *and
there remained no strength in me*: for my comeliness was
turned in me into corruption, and I retained no strength.
Yet heard I the voice of His words: and when I heard the
voice of His words, then was I in a deep sleep *on my face,
and my face towards the ground*" (Dan. 10: 6-9). Once more,
then, we are shown that a sight of the Sovereign God causes
creature strength to wither up, and results in man being
humbled into the dust before his Maker. What then ought
to be our attitude toward the Supreme Sovereign? We reply,

1. ONE OF GODLY FEAR.

Why is it that, today, the masses are so utterly uncon-
cerned about spiritual and eternal things, and that they are
lovers of pleasures more than lovers of God? Why is it that
even on the battlefields multitudes were so indifferent to
their souls' welfare? Why is it that defiance of heaven is becoming more open, more blatant, more daring? The answer
is, "There is no fear of God before their eyes" (Rom. 3: 18).
Again; why is it that the authority of the Scriptures has been
lowered so sadly of late? Why is it that even among those
who profess to be the Lord's people there is so little subjection to His Word, and that its precepts are so lightly esteemed
and so readily set aside? Ah! what needs to be stressed today is that God is a *God to be feared*.

"The *fear of the Lord* is the beginning of knowledge"
(Pro. 1: 7). Happy the soul that has been awed by a view of
God's majesty, that has had a vision of God's awful greatness,
His ineffable holiness, His perfect righteousness, His irresistible power, His sovereign grace. Does someone say, "But
it is only the unsaved, those *outside* of Christ, who need to
fear God"? Then the sufficient answer is that the saved,
those who are *in Christ*, are admonished to work out their
own salvation with "fear and trembling." Time was, when

it was the general custom to speak of a believer as a "God-fearing man"—that such an appellation has become nearly extinct only serves to show whither we have drifted. Nevertheless, it still stands written, "Like as a father pitieth his children, so the Lord pitieth them that *fear* Him" (Ps. 103: 13)!

When we speak of godly fear, of course, we do not mean a servile fear, such as prevails among the heathen in connection with their gods. No; we mean that spirit which Jehovah is pledged to bless, that spirit to which the prophet referred when he said, "To this man will I (the Lord) look, even to him that is poor and of a contrite spirit, *and trembleth at My Word*" (Isa. 66: 2). It was this the apostle had in view when he wrote, "Honour all men. Love the brotherhood. *Fear God.* Honour the king" (1 Pet. 2: 17). And nothing will foster this godly fear like a recognition of the sovereign Majesty of God.

What ought to be our attitude toward the Sovereignty of God? We answer again,

2. ONE OF IMPLICIT OBEDIENCE.

A sight of God leads to a realization of our littleness and nothingness, and issues in a sense of dependency and of casting ourselves upon God. Or, again; a view of the Divine Majesty promotes the spirit of godly fear, and this, in turn, begets an obedient walk. Here then is the Divine antidote for the native evil of our hearts. Naturally, man is filled with a sense of his own importance, with his greatness and self-sufficiency; in a word, with pride and rebellion. But, as we remarked, the great corrective is to behold the Mighty God, for this alone will really humble him. Man will glory either in himself or in God. Man will live either to serve and please himself, or he will seek to serve and please the Lord. None can serve two masters.

Irreverence begets disobedience. Said the haughty monarch of Egypt, "Who is the Lord that I should obey His voice to let Israel go? *I know not the Lord*, neither will I let Israel go" (Ex. 5: 2). To Pharaoh, the God of the Hebrews was merely *a* god, one among many, a powerless entity who needed not to be feared or served. How sadly mistaken he was, and how bitterly he had to pay for his mistake, he soon discovered; but what we are here seeking to emphasize is, that Pharaoh's defiant spirit was the fruit of irreverence, and this irreverence was the consequence of *his ignorance* of the majesty and authority of the Divine Being.

Now if irreverence begets disobedience, true reverence will produce and promote obedience. To realize that the Holy Scriptures are a revelation from the Most High, communicating to us His mind and defining for us His will, is the first step toward practical godliness. To recognize that the Bible is *God's* Word, and that its precepts are the precepts of the Almighty, will lead us to see what an awful thing it is to despise and ignore them. To receive the Bible as addressed to our own souls, given to us by the Creator Himself, will cause us to cry with the Psalmist, "*Incline my heart unto Thy testimonies. . . . Order my steps in Thy Word*" (Ps. 119: 36, 133). Once the sovereignty of the Author of the Word is apprehended, it will no longer be a matter of picking and choosing from the precepts and statutes of that Word, selecting those which meet with our approval; but it will be seen that nothing less than an unqualified and whole-hearted submission is becoming to the creature.

What ought to be our attitude towards the Sovereignty of God? We answer, once more,

3. One of entire resignation.

A true recognition of God's Sovereignty will exclude all *murmuring*. This is self-evident, yet the thought deserves to be dwelt upon. It is natural to murmur against afflictions and losses. It is natural to complain when we are deprived of those things upon which we had set our hearts. We are apt to regard our possessions as ours unconditionally. We feel that, when we have prosecuted our plans with prudence and diligence, we are *entitled* to success; that when by dint of hard work we have accumulated a "competence," we *deserve* to keep and enjoy it; that when we are surrounded by a happy family, no power may lawfully enter the charmed circle and strike down a loved one; and if, in any of these cases, disappointment, bankruptcy, death, actually comes, the perverted instinct of the human heart is to cry out against God. But in the one who, by grace, has recognized God's sovereignty, such murmuring is silenced, and instead, there is a bowing to the Divine will, and an acknowledgement that He has not afflicted us as sorely as we *deserve*.

A true recognition of God's sovereignty will avow God's perfect right to do with us as He wills. The one who bows to the pleasure of the Almighty will acknowledge His absolute right to do with us as seemeth Him good. If He chooses to send poverty, sickness, domestic bereavements, even while the heart is bleeding at every pore, it will say, Shall not the Judge of all the earth do right! Often there will be a struggle, for the carnal mind remains in the believer to the end of his earthly pilgrimage. But though there may be a conflict within his breast, nevertheless, to the one who has really yielded himself to this blessed truth, there will presently be heard that Voice saying, as of old it said to the turbulent Gennesaret, " Peace, be still "; and the tempestuous flood within will be quieted, and the subdued soul will lift a tearful but confident eye to heaven and say, " Thy will be done."

A striking illustration of a soul bowing to the sovereign will of God is furnished by the history of Eli the high priest of Israel. In 1 Samuel 3 we learn how God revealed to the child Samuel that He was about to slay Eli's two sons for their wickedness, and on the morrow Samuel communicates this message to the aged priest. It is difficult to conceive of more appalling intelligence for the heart of a pious parent. The announcement that his child is going to be stricken down by sudden death is, under any circumstances, a great trial to any father, but to learn that his two sons—in the prime of their manhood, but utterly *unprepared* to die— were to be cut off by a Divine judgment, must have been overwhelming. Yet what was the effect upon Eli when he learned from Samuel the tragic tidings? What reply did he make when he heard the awful news? "And he said, It is the Lord: *let Him do what seemeth Him good*" (1 Sam. 3: 18). And not another word escaped him. Wonderful submission! Sublime resignation! Lovely exemplification of the power of Divine grace to control the strongest affections of the human heart and subdue the rebellious will, bringing it into unrepining acquiescence to the sovereign pleasure of Jehovah.

Another example, equally striking, is seen in the life of Job. As is well known, Job was one that feared God and eschewed evil. If ever there was one who might reasonably expect Divine providence to smile upon him—we speak as a man—it was Job. Yet, how fared it with him? For a time, the lines fell unto him in pleasant places. The Lord filled his quiver by giving him seven sons and three daughters. He prospered him in his temporal affairs until he owned great possessions. But of a sudden, the sun of life was hidden behind dark clouds. In a single day Job lost not only his flocks and herds, but his sons and daughters as well. News arrived that his cattle had been carried off by robbers, and his children slain by a cyclone. And how did he receive this intelligence? Hearken to his sublime words: "*The Lord* gave, and *the Lord* hath taken away." He bowed to the sovereign will of Jehovah. He traced his afflictions back to their First Cause. He looked behind the Sabeans who had stolen his cattle, and beyond the winds that had destroyed his children, and *saw the hand of God*. But not only did Job *recognize* God's sovereignty, he *rejoiced* in it, too. To the words, "The Lord gave, and the Lord hath taken away," he added, "*Blessed be the name of the Lord*" (Job 1: 21). Again we say, Sweet submission! Sublime resignation!

A true recognition of God's sovereignty causes us to hold our every plan in abeyance to God's will. The writer well recalls an incident in England early in the present century. Queen Victoria was dead, and the date for the coronation of her eldest son, Edward, had been set for April, 1902. In all the announcements which were sent out, two little letters were omitted—D. V.—Deo Volente: God willing. Plans were made and all arrangements completed for the imposing celebrations suitable to the great occasion. Kings and emperors from all parts of the earth had received invitations to attend the royal ceremony. The Prince's proclamations were printed and displayed, but, so far as the writer is aware, the letters D. V. were not found on a single one of them. A most imposing programme had been arranged, and the late Queen's eldest son was to be crowned Edward the Seventh at Westminster Abbey at a certain hour on a fixed day. *And then God intervened,* and all man's plans were frustrated. A still small voice was heard to say, "You have reckoned without Me," and Prince Edward was stricken down with appendicitis, and his coronation postponed for months!

As remarked, a true recognition of God's sovereignty causes us to hold *our* plans in abeyance to God's will. It makes us recognize that the Divine Potter has absolute power over the clay and moulds it according to his own imperial pleasure. It causes us to heed that admonition—now, alas! so generally disregarded—"Go to now, ye that say, Today or tomorrow *we will* go into such a city, and continue there a year, and buy and sell, and get gain: Whereas ye know not what shall be on the morrow. For what is your life? It is even a vapour, that appeareth for a little time, and then vanisheth away. For that ye *ought* to say, *If the Lord will,* we shall live, and do this, or that" (Jas. 4: 13-15). Yes, it is to the *Lord's will* we must bow. It is for *Him* to say where I shall live—whether in this place or in that (Acts 17: 26). It is for *Him* to determine under what circumstances I shall live—whether amid wealth or poverty, whether in health or sickness. It is for *Him* to say how long I shall live—whether I shall be cut down in youth like the flower of the field, or whether I shall continue for three score and ten years. *Really* to learn this lesson is, by grace, to attain unto a high form in the school of God, and even when we think we have learnt it, we discover, again and again, that we have to relearn it.

4. ONE OF DEEP THANKFULNESS AND JOY.

The *heart's* apprehension of this most blessed truth of the sovereignty of God produces something far different from a sullen bowing to the inevitable. The philosophy of this perishing world knows nothing better than to "make the best of a bad job." But with the Christian it should be far otherwise. Not only should the recognition of God's supremacy beget within us godly fear, implicit obedience, and entire resignation, but it should cause us to say with the Psalmist, "Bless the Lord, O my soul: and all that is within me, bless His holy name." Does not the apostle say, "Giving thanks *always* for all things unto God and the Father in the name of our Lord Jesus Christ" (Eph. 5: 20)? Ah, it is at *this* point that the state of our souls is so often put to the test. Alas, there is so much self-will in each of us. When things go as *we* wish them, we appear to be very grateful to God; but what of those occasions when things go contrary to our plans and desires?

We take it for granted, when the real Christian takes a train-journey, that, upon reaching his destination, he devoutly returns thanks unto God—which, of course, argues that *He* controls everything; otherwise, we ought to thank the engine-driver, the stoker, the signalmen, and others. Or, if in business, at the close of a good week, gratitude is expressed unto the Giver of every good (temporal) and of every perfect (spiritual) gift—which again, argues that *He* directs all customers to your shop. So far, so good. Such examples occasion no difficulty. But imagine the opposites. Suppose my train was delayed for hours; suppose another train ran into it, and I am injured! Or, suppose I have had a poor week in business, or that lightning struck my shop and set it on fire, or that burglars broke in and rifled it—then what: do I see the hand of God in *these* things?

Take the case of Job once more. When loss after loss came his way, what did he do? Bemoan his "bad luck"? Curse the robbers? Murmur against God? No; he bowed before Him in worship. Ah, dear reader, there is no real rest for your poor heart until you learn to see the hand of God in everything. But for that, *faith* must be in constant exercise.

And what is faith? A blind credulity? A fatalistic acquiescence? No, far from it. Faith is a resting on the sure Word
of the living God, and therefore it says, " We *know* that all
things work together for good to them that love God, to
them who are the called according to His purpose " (Rom.
8: 28); and therefore faith will give thanks "always for all
things." Operative faith will " Rejoice in the Lord *alway* "
(Phil. 4: 4).

We turn now to mark how this recognition of God's sovereignty which is expressed in godly fear, implicit obedience,
entire resignation, and deep thankfulness and joy was supremely and perfectly exemplified by the Lord Jesus Christ.
In all things the Lord Jesus has left us an example that we
should follow His steps. But is this true in connection with
the first point made above? Are the words "godly fear" ever
linked with His peerless name? Remembering that "godly
fear" signifies not a servile terror, but rather a filial subjection and reverence, and remembering too that "the fear of
the Lord is the beginning of wisdom," would it not rather
be strange if no mention at all were made of "godly fear"
in connection with the One who was wisdom incarnate!
What a wonderful and precious word is that of Heb. 5: 7—
" Who in the days of His flesh, having offered up prayers
and supplications with strong crying and tears unto Him
that was able to save Him from death, and having been
heard *for His godly fear* . . ." (R.V.). What was it but " *godly*
fear " which caused the Lord Jesus to be "subject" unto
Mary and Joseph in the days of His childhood? Was it not
" godly fear "—a filial subjection to and reverence for God—
that we see displayed, when we read, "And He came to
Nazareth where He had been brought up: and, *as His custom was,* He went into the synagogue on the Sabbath day "
(Luke 4: 16)? Was it not "godly fear" which caused the
incarnate Son to say, when tempted by Satan to fall down
and worship him, "It is written, thou shalt worship *the
Lord thy God* and Him only shalt thou serve "? Was it not
" godly fear " which moved Him to say to the cleansed leper,
" Go thy way, shew thyself to the priest, and offer the gift

that Moses *commanded*" (Matt. 8: 4)? But why multiply illustrations?[1]

How perfect was the *obedience* that the Lord Jesus offered to God the Father! And in reflecting upon this let us not lose sight of that wondrous grace which caused Him, who was in the very form of God, to stoop so low as to take upon Him the form of a *Servant,* and thus be brought into the place where obedience was becoming. As the perfect Servant He yielded complete obedience to His Father. How absolute and entire that obedience was we may learn from the words, He " became *obedient unto death,* even the death of the Cross " (Phil. 2: 8). That this was a conscious and intelligent obedience is clear from His own language—" Therefore doth My Father love Me, because I lay down My life, that I might take it again. No man taketh it from Me, but I lay it down of Myself. I have power to lay it down, and I have power to take it again. *This commandment* have I received of My Father " (John 10: 17, 18).

And what shall we say of the absolute *resignation* of the Son to the Father's will—what, but that between Them there was entire oneness of accord. Said He, " For I came down from heaven, not to do Mine own will, but the will of Him that sent Me " (John 6: 38), and how fully He substantiated that claim all know who have attentively followed His path as marked out in the Scriptures. Behold Him in Gethsemane! The bitter " cup," held in the Father's hand, is presented to His view. Mark well His attitude. *Learn* of Him who was meek and lowly in heart. Remember that there in the garden we see the Word become flesh—a perfect Man. His body is quivering at every nerve, in contemplation of the physical sufferings which await Him; His holy and sensitive nature is shrinking from the horrible indignities which shall be heaped upon Him; His heart is breaking at the awful " reproach " which is before Him; His spirit is greatly troubled as He foresees the terrible conflict with the Power of Dark-

[1] Note how Old Testament prophecy also declared that "the Spirit of the Lord" should "rest upon Him, the spirit of wisdom and understanding, the spirit of counsel and might, the spirit of knowledge and of *the fear of the Lord*" (Isa. 11: 1, 2).

ness; and above all, and supremely, His soul is filled with horror at the thought of being separated from God Himself —thus and there He pours out His soul to the Father, and with strong crying and tears He sheds, as it were, great drops of blood. And now observe and listen. Still the beating of your heart, and hearken to the words which fall from His blessed lips—" Father, if *Thou* be willing, remove this cup from Me: *nevertheless*, not My will, but *Thine* be done" (Luke 22 : 42). Here is submission personified. Here is resignation to the pleasure of a sovereign God superlatively exemplified. And He has left us an example that we should follow His steps. He who was God became man, and was tempted in all points like as we are—sin apart—to show us *how* to wear *our* creature nature!

Above, we asked, What shall we say of Christ's absolute resignation to the Father's will? We answer further, that here, as everywhere, He was unique, peerless. In all things He has the pre-eminence. In the Lord Jesus there was no rebellious will to be broken. In His heart there was nothing to be subdued. Was not this one reason why, in the language of prophecy, He said, " I am a worm, and no man " (Ps. 22 : 6)—*a worm has no power of resistance!* It was because in Him there *was* no resistance that He could say, " *My meat* is to do the will of Him that sent Me" (John 4 : 34). Yea, it was because He was in perfect accord with the Father in all things that He said, " *I delight* to do Thy will, O my God; yea, Thy law is within My heart " (Ps. 40 : 8). Note the last clause here and behold *His* matchless excellency. God has to *put* His laws into *our* minds, and *write* them in *our* hearts (see Heb. 8 : 10), but His law was *already* in *Christ's* heart!

What a beautiful and striking illustration of Christ's thankfulness and joy is found in Matt. 11. There we behold, first, the weakness in the faith of His forerunner (vers. 22, 23). Next, we learn of the discontent of the people: satisfied neither with Christ's joyous message, nor with John's solemn one (vers. 16-20). Third, we have the non-repentance of those favoured cities in which our Lord's mightiest works

were done (vers. 21-24). And then we read, " *At that time*
Jesus answered and said, I *thank* Thee, O Father, Lord of
heaven and earth, because Thou hast hid these things from
the wise and prudent, and hast revealed them unto babes "
(ver. 25)! Note that the parallel passage in Luke 11 opens
by saying, " In that hour Jesus *rejoiced* in spirit, and said,
I thank Thee," etc. Ah, here was submission in its purest
form. Here was One by whom the worlds were made, yet,
in the days of His humiliation, and in the face of His rejection, thankfully and joyously bowing to the will of the
" Lord of heaven and earth."

What ought to be our attitude towards God's sovereignty?
Finally,

5. ONE OF ADORING WORSHIP.

It has been well said that " true worship is based upon
recognized GREATNESS, and greatness is superlatively seen
in Sovereignty, and at no other footstool will men *really*
worship" (J. B. Moody). In the presence of the Divine
King upon His throne even the seraphim " veil their
faces."

Divine sovereignty is not the sovereignty of a tyrannical
Despot, but the exercised pleasure of One who is infinitely
wise and good! Because God is infinitely wise He *cannot*
err, and because He is infinitely righteous He *will not* do
wrong. Here then is the *preciousness* of this truth. The
mere fact itself that God's will is irresistible and irreversible
fills me with fear, but once I realize that God wills only that
which is good, my heart is made to rejoice.

Here then is the final answer to the question of this chapter—What ought to be our attitude toward the sovereignty
of God? The becoming attitude for us to take is that of
godly fear, implicit obedience, and unreserved resignation
and submission. But not only so: the recognition of the
sovereignty of God, and the realization that the Sovereign
Himself is my *Father*, ought to overwhelm the heart and
cause me to bow before Him in adoring worship. At all
times I must say, " Even so, Father, for *so* it seemeth *good* in

Thy sight." We conclude with an example which well illustrates our meaning.

Some two hundred years ago the saintly Madame Guyon,
after ten years spent in a dungeon lying far below the surface of the ground, and lit only by a candle at meal-times,
wrote these words,

> "A little bird I am,
> Shut from the fields of air;
> Yet in my cage I sit and sing
> To Him who placed me there;
> Well pleased a prisoner to be,
> *Because, my God, it pleases Thee.*
>
> Nought have I else to do;
> I sing the whole day long;
> And He whom most I love to please,
> Doth listen to my song;
> He caught and bound my wandering wing
> But still He bends to hear me sing.
>
> My cage confines me round;
> Abroad I cannot fly;
> But though my wing is closely bound,
> My heart's at liberty.
> My prison walls cannot control
> The flight, the freedom of the soul.
>
> Ah; it is good to soar
> These bolts and bars above,
> To Him *whose purpose I adore,*
> Whose Providence I love;
> And in Thy mighty will to find
> The joy, the freedom of the mind."

THE VALUE OF THIS DOCTRINE

" All Scripture is given by inspiration of God,
  And is profitable for doctrine,
  For reproof, for correction, for instruction in righteousness:
  That the man of God may be perfect,
  Throughly furnished unto all good works " (2 Tim. 3:16, 17).

" ALL Scripture is given by inspiration of God, and *is pro-fitable for doctrine,* for reproof, for correction, for instruction in righteousness: that the man of God may be perfect, throughly furnished unto all good works " (2 Tim. 3: 16, 17). " Doctrine " means " teaching," and it is by doctrine or teaching that the great realities of God and of our relation to Him—of Christ, the Spirit, salvation, grace, glory, are made known to us. It is by doctrine (through the power of the Spirit) that believers are nourished and edified, and where doctrine is neglected, growth in grace and effective witnessing for Christ necessarily cease. How sad then that doctrine is now decried as " unpractical " when, in fact, doctrine is the very basis of the practical life. There is an inseparable connection between belief and practice—" *As* he thinketh in his heart, *so* is he " (Pro. 23: 7). The relation between Divine truth and Christian character is that of cause to effect—" And ye shall *know* the truth, *and* the truth shall make you free " (John 8: 32)—free from ignorance, free from prejudice, free from error, free from the wiles of Satan, free from the power of evil; and if the truth is not " known " then such freedom will not be enjoyed. Observe the *order* of mention in the passage with which we have opened. All Scripture is profitable *first* for " doctrine "! The same order is observed throughout the Epistles, particularly in the great doctrinal treatises of the apostle Paul. Read the Epistle of " Romans " and it will be found that there is not a single admonition in the first five chapters. In the Epistle of

" Ephesians " there are no exhortations till the fourth chapter is reached. The order is first doctrinal exposition and then admonition or exhortation for the regulation of the daily walk.

The substitution of so-called " practical " preaching for the doctrinal exposition which it has supplanted is the root cause of many of the evil maladies which now afflict the church of God. The reason why there is so little depth, so little intelligence, so little grasp of the fundamental verities of Christianity, is because so few believers have been established in the faith through hearing the doctrines of grace expounded, and through their own personal study of them. While the soul is unestablished in the doctrine of the Divine Inspiration of the Scriptures—their full and verbal inspiration—there can be no firm foundation for faith to rest upon. While the soul is ignorant of the doctrine of Justification, there can be no real and intelligent assurance of its acceptance in the Beloved. While the soul is unacquainted with the teaching of the Word upon Sanctification, it is open to receive all the errors of Perfectionism or other wrong teaching. And so we might go on right through the entire range of Christian doctrine. It is *ignorance* of doctrine that has rendered the professing church helpless to cope with the rising tide of infidelity. It is *ignorance* of doctrine which is mainly responsible for thousands of professing Christians being captivated by the numerous false " isms " of the day. It is because the time has now arrived when the bulk of our churches " *will not endure* sound doctrine " (2 Tim. 4: 3) that they so readily receive *false* doctrines. Of course it is true that doctrine, like anything else in Scripture, may be studied from a merely cold intellectual viewpoint, and *thus* approached, doctrinal teaching and doctrinal study will leave the *heart* untouched, and will naturally be " dry " and profitless. But doctrine properly received, doctrine studied with an *exercised* heart, will ever lead into a deeper knowledge of God and of the unsearchable riches of Christ.

The doctrine of God's sovereignty then is no mere metaphysical dogma which is devoid of practical value, but is one that is calculated to produce a powerful effect upon Christian character and the daily walk. The doctrine of God's sovereignty lies at the foundation of Christian theology, and in importance is perhaps second only to the Divine Inspiration of the Scriptures. It is the centre of gravity in the system of Christian truth; the sun around which all the lesser orbs are grouped; the cord upon which all other doctrines are strung like so many pearls, holding them in place and giving them unity. It is the plumbline by which every creed needs to be tested; the balance in which every human dogma must be weighed. It is designed as the sheet-anchor for our souls amid the storms of life. The doctrine of God's sovereignty is a Divine cordial to refresh our spirits. It is designed and adapted to mould the affections of the heart, and to give a right direction to conduct. It produces gratitude in prosperity and patience in adversity. It affords comfort for the present and a sense of security respecting the unknown future. It is, and it does, all and much more than we have just said, because it ascribes to God—the Father, the Son, and the Holy Spirit—the glory which is His due, and places the creature in his proper place before Him—in the dust.

We shall now consider the value of the doctrine in detail.

1. IT DEEPENS OUR VENERATION OF THE DIVINE CHARACTER.

The doctrine of God's sovereignty as it is unfolded in the Scriptures affords an exalted view of the Divine perfections. It maintains *His rights* as Creator. It insists that " to us there is but one God, the Father, *of whom are all things,* and we in Him; and one Lord Jesus Christ, *by whom are all things,* and we by Him" (1 Cor. 8: 6). It declares that His rights are those of the " potter " who forms and fashions the clay into vessels of whatever type and for whatever use He may please. Its testimony is, " Thou hast created all things, *and for Thy pleasure* they are and were created " (Rev. 4: 11). It argues that none has any right to "reply" against God, and that the only becoming attitude for the creature to take is one of reverent submission before Him. Thus the apprehension of the absolute supremacy of God is of great

practical importance, for unless we have a proper regard to
His high sovereignty He will never be honoured in our
thoughts of Him, nor will He have His proper place in our
hearts and lives.

It exhibits the *inscrutableness of His wisdom*. It shows
that while God is infinite in His *holiness,* He has permitted
evil to enter His fair creation; that while He is the Possessor
of *all power,* He has allowed the Devil to wage war *against
Him* for six thousand years at least; that while He is the
perfect embodiment of *love,* He spared not His own Son; that
while He is the God of *all grace,* not all are made partakers
of that grace. High mysteries are these. Scripture does not
deny them, but acknowledges their existence—" O the depth
of the riches both of the wisdom and knowledge of God ! how
unsearchable are His judgments, and His ways *past finding
out*!" (Rom. 11:33).

It makes known the *irreversibleness of His will.* " Known
unto God are all His works from the beginning of the world "
(Acts 15:18). From the beginning God purposed to glorify
Himself " in the Church by Christ Jesus, throughout all ages,
world without end " (Eph. 3:21). To this end, He created
the world, and formed man. His all-wise plan was not defeated when man fell, for in the Lamb " slain from the
foundation of the world" (Rev. 13:8) we behold the Fall
anticipated. Nor will God's purpose be thwarted by the
wickedness of men since the Fall, as is clear from the words
of the Psalmist, " *Surely the wrath of man shall praise Thee*:
the remainder of wrath shalt Thou restrain " (Ps. 76:10).
Because God is the Almighty His will cannot be withstood.
" His purposes originated in eternity, and are carried forward without change to eternity. They extend to all His
works, and control all events. He 'worketh all things after
the counsel of His own will.' " (Dr. Rice). Neither man nor
devil can successfully resist Him, therefore is it written,
" The Lord reigneth; *let the people tremble* " (Ps. 99:1).

It magnifies *His grace.* Grace is unmerited favour, and
because grace is shown to the undeserving and Hell-deserving, to those who have *no claim* upon God, therefore is grace

free and can be manifested toward the chief of sinners. But because grace is exercised toward those who are *destitute* of worthiness or merit, grace is *sovereign;* that is to say, God bestows grace upon whom He pleases. Divine sovereignty has ordained that *some* shall be condemned for their sins to show that *all* deserved such an end. But grace intervenes and draws out from a lost humanity a people for God's name, to be throughout all eternity the monuments of His inscrutable favour. Sovereign grace reveals God breaking down the opposition of the human heart, subduing the enmity of the carnal mind, and bringing us to love Him because He first loved us.

2. IT IS THE SOLID FOUNDATION OF ALL TRUE RELIGION.

This naturally follows from what we have said above under the first head. If the doctrine of Divine sovereignty alone gives God His rightful place, then it is also true that it alone can supply a firm base for practical religion to build upon. There can be no progress in Divine things until there is the personal recognition that God is Supreme, that He is to be feared and revered, that He is to be owned and served *as Lord*. We read the Scriptures in vain unless we come to them earnestly desiring a better knowledge of God's will for us—any other motive is selfish and utterly inadequate and unworthy. Every prayer we send up to God is but carnal presumption unless it be offered " according to *His* will "— anything short of this is to ask " amiss," that we might consume upon our *own* lusts the things requested. Every service we engage in is but a " dead work " unless it be done for the glory of God. Experimental religion consists mainly in the perception and performance of the Divine will—performance both active and passive. We are predestinated to be " conformed to the image of God's son," whose meat it ever was to do the will of the One that sent Him, and the measure in which each saint is becoming " conformed " practically, in his daily life, is largely determined by his response to our Lord's word—" Take My yoke upon you, *and learn of Me*; for I am meek and lowly in heart."

3. It repudiates the heresy of salvation by works.

"There is a way which seemeth right unto a man; but the end thereof are the ways of death" (Pro. 14:12). The way which "*seemeth right*" and which ends in "*death*," death eternal, is salvation by human effort and merit. The belief in salvation by works is one that is common to human nature. It may not always assume the grosser form of Popish penances, or even of Protestant "repentance"—i.e., sorrowing for sin, which is never the full meaning of repentance in Scripture. Anything which gives man a place at all is but a variety of the same evil genus. To say, as alas! many preachers are saying, God is willing to do His part if you will do yours, is a wretched and excuseless *denial* of the Gospel of His grace. To declare that God helps those who help themselves, is to *repudiate* one of the most precious truths taught in the Bible, and in the Bible alone; namely, that God helps those who are *unable* to help themselves, who have tried again and again, only to fail. To say that the sinner's salvation turns upon the action of his *own* will, is another form of the God-dishonouring dogma of salvation by human efforts. In the final analysis, any movement of the will is a work: it is something *from me*, something which *I do*. But the doctrine of God's sovereignty lays the axe at the root of this evil tree by declaring, "*It is not of him that willeth, nor* of him that runneth, but of God that sheweth mercy*" (Rom. 9:16). Does some one say, Such a doctrine will drive sinners to *despair*. The reply is, Be it so; it is just such despair the writer longs to see prevail. It is not until the sinner despairs of any help from himself, that he will ever fall into the arms of sovereign mercy; but if once the Holy Spirit convicts him that there is *no help* in himself, then he will recognize that he is *lost*, and will cry, "God be merciful to me a sinner," and *such* a cry will be heard. If the author may be allowed to bear personal witness, he has found during the course of his ministry that the sermons he has preached on human depravity, the sinner's helplessness to do *anything* himself, and the salvation of the soul turning upon the sovereign mercy of God, have been those most owned and blessed in the salvation of the lost. We repeat, then, a sense of utter *helplessness* is the first prerequisite to any sound conversion. There is no salvation for any soul until it looks away from itself, looks to something, yea, to Someone, *outside* of itself.

4. IT IS DEEPLY HUMBLING TO THE CREATURE.

This doctrine of the absolute sovereignty of God is a great battering-ram against human pride, and in this it is in sharp contrast with "the doctrines of men." The spirit of our age is essentially that of boasting and glorying in the flesh. The achievements of man, his development and progress, his greatness and self-sufficiency, are the shrine at which the world worships today. But the truth of God's sovereignty, with all its corollaries, removes every ground for human boasting and instills the spirit of humility in its stead. It declares that salvation is of the Lord—of the Lord in its origination, in its operation, and in its consummation. It insists that the Lord has to apply as well as supply, that He has to complete as well as begin His saving work in our souls, that He has not only to reclaim but to maintain and sustain us to the end. It teaches that salvation is by grace through faith, and that *all* our works (before conversion), good as well as evil, count for nothing toward salvation. It tells us we are "born, not of the will of the flesh, nor of the will of man, but of God" (John 1: 13). And all this is most humbling to the heart of man, who wants to contribute something to the price of his redemption and do that which will afford ground for boasting and self-satisfaction.

But if this doctrine humbles *us*, it results in praise to *God*. If, in the light of God's sovereignty, we have seen our own worthlessness and helplessness, we shall indeed cry with the Psalmist, "*All* my springs are *in Thee*" (Ps. 87: 7). If by nature we were "children of wrath," and by practice rebels against the Divine government and justly exposed to the "curse" of the Law, and if God was under *no* obligation to rescue us from the fiery indignation, and yet, notwithstanding, He delivered up His well-beloved Son for *us* all; then how such grace and love will melt our hearts! how the apprehension of it will cause us to say in adoring gratitude, "*Not unto us*, O Lord, not unto us, *but unto Thy name give glory*, for Thy mercy, and for Thy truth's sake" (Ps. 115: 1)! How readily shall each of us acknowledge, "*By the grace of God* I am what I am"! With that wondering praise shall we exclaim—

> "Why was I *made* to hear His voice,
> And enter while there's room,
> When thousands make a wretched choice,
> And rather starve than come?
> 'Twas the same love that spread the feast,
> That sweetly *forced* us in;
> Else we had still refused to taste
> And perished in our sin."
>
> (ISAAC WATTS)

5. IT AFFORDS A SENSE OF ABSOLUTE SECURITY.

God is infinite in power, and therefore it is impossible to withstand His will or resist the outworking of His decrees. Such a statement as that is well calculated to fill the sinner with alarm, but from the saint it evokes naught but praise. Let us add a word and see what a difference it makes: —*My* God is infinite in power! *then* "I will not fear what man can do unto me." My God is infinite in power, *then* "what time I am afraid I will trust in Thee." My God is infinite in power, *then* "I will both lay me down in peace, and sleep: for Thou, Lord, *only* makest me dwell in safety" (Ps. 4: 8). Right down the ages *this* has been the source of the saints' confidence. Was not this the assurance of Moses when, in his parting words to Israel, he said—"There is none like unto the God of Jeshurun (Israel), who rideth upon the heaven in thy help, and in His excellency on the sky. The eternal God is thy refuge, *and underneath are the everlasting arms*" (Deut. 33: 26, 27)? Was it not this sense of security that caused the Psalmist, moved by the Holy Spirit, to write —"He that dwelleth in the secret place of the Most High shall abide under the shadow of the Almighty. I will say of the Lord, *He is my refuge and my fortress: my God: in Him will I trust. Surely* He shall deliver thee from the snare of the fowler, and from the noisome pestilence. He shall cover thee with His feathers, and under His wings shalt thou trust: His truth shall be thy shield and buckler. *Thou shalt not be afraid* for the terror by night; nor for the arrow that flieth by day; nor for the pestilence that walketh in darkness; nor for the destruction that wasteth at noonday. A thousand shall fall at thy side, and ten thousand at thy right hand, *but it shall not come nigh thee* ... Because thou hast made the Lord, which is my refuge, even the Most High *thy habitation;* there shall no evil befall thee [instead, all things will work together for *good*], neither shall any plague come nigh thy dwelling" (Ps. 91)?

> "Plagues and deaths around me fly;
> Till He bids, I cannot die;
> Not a single shaft can hit,
> Till the God of love sees fit."
> (JOHN RYLAND)

O the preciousness of this truth! Here am I, a poor, helpless, senseless "sheep," yet am I *secure* in the hand of Christ. And why am I secure *there*? None can pluck me thence *because* the hand that holds me is that of the Son of God, and all power in heaven and earth is *His!* Again; I have no strength of my own: the world, the flesh, and the Devil, are arrayed against me, so I commit myself into the care and keeping of the Lord and say with the apostle, "I know Whom I have believed, and am persuaded *that He is able* to keep that which I have committed unto Him against that day" (2 Tim. 1: 12). And what is the ground of my confidence? *How* do *I know* that He is able to keep that which I have committed unto Him? I know it because God is *almighty*, the King of kings and Lord of lords.

6. IT SUPPLIES COMFORT IN SORROW.

The doctrine of God's sovereignty is one that is full of consolation and imparts great peace to the Christian. The sovereignty of God is a foundation that nothing can shake and is more firm than the heavens and earth. How blessed to know there is no corner of the universe that is out of His reach! as said the Psalmist, " Whither shall I go from Thy Spirit? *or whither shall I flee from Thy presence?* If I ascend up into heaven, *Thou art there*: if I make my bed in hell, behold, *Thou art there.* If I take the wings of the morning, and dwell in the uttermost parts of the sea: *even there shall Thy hand lead me,* and Thy right hand shall hold me. If I say, Surely the darkness shall cover me; *even the night shall be light about me.* Yea, the darkness hideth not from Thee: but the night shineth as the day: the darkness and the light are both alike to Thee " (Ps. 139: 7-12). How blessed it is to know that God's strong hand is upon every one and every thing! How blessed to know that not a sparrow falls to the ground without His notice! How blessed to know that our very *afflictions* come not by chance, nor from the Devil, but are ordained and ordered *by God*: — " That no man should be moved by these afflictions: for yourselves *know* that we are *appointed* thereunto " (1 Thess. 3: 3)!

But our God is not only infinite in power, He is infinite in wisdom and goodness too. And herein is the preciousness of this truth. God wills only that which is good, and His will is irreversible and irresistible! God is too wise to err and too loving to cause His child a needless tear. Therefore, if God be perfect wisdom and perfect goodness, how blessed is the assurance that everything *is* in *His* hand, and moulded by His will according to His eternal purpose! " *Behold, He taketh away,* who can hinder Him? who will say unto Him what doest Thou?" (Job 9: 12). Yet, how comforting to learn that *it is* " He," and not the Devil, who " taketh away " our loved ones! Ah! what peace for our poor frail hearts to be told that the number of our days is with Him (Job 7: 1; 14: 5); that disease and death are His messengers, and always march under *His* orders; that it is the Lord who gives and the Lord who takes away!

7. IT BEGETS A SPIRIT OF SWEET RESIGNATION.

To bow before the sovereign will of God is one of the

great secrets of peace and happiness. There can be no real submission, with contentment, until we are broken in spirit, that is, until we are willing and *glad* for the Lord to have *His* way with us. Not that we are insisting upon a spirit of *fatalistic acquiescence*; far from it. The saints are exhorted to "*prove* what is that *good*, and *acceptable*, and *perfect will of God*" (Rom. 12:2).

We touched upon this subject of resignation to God's will in the previous chapter, and there, in addition to the supreme Pattern, we cited the example of Eli and Job: we would now supplement their cases with further examples. What a word is that in Lev. 10:3—"And Aaron held his peace." Look at the circumstances: "And Nadab and Abihu, the sons of Aaron, took either of them his censer, and put fire therein, and put incense thereon, and offered strange fire before the Lord, which He commanded them not. And there went out fire from the Lord, and devoured them, and they died before the Lord. . . . *And Aaron held his peace.*" Two of the high priest's sons were slain, slain by a visitation of *Divine judgment*, and they were probably *intoxicated* at the time; moreover, this trial came upon Aaron *suddenly*, without anything to *prepare* him for it; yet he "held his peace." Precious exemplification of the power of God's all-sufficient grace!

Consider now an utterance which fell from the lips of David: "And the king said unto Zadok, Carry back the ark of God into the city: if I shall find favour in the eyes of the Lord, He will bring me again, and shew me both it, and His habitation. But if He thus say, I have no delight in thee; behold, here am I, *let Him do to me as seemeth good unto Him*" (2 Sam. 15:25, 26). Here, too, the circumstances which confronted the speaker were exceedingly trying to the human heart. David was sore pressed with sorrow. His own son was driving him from the throne, and seeking his very life. Whether he would ever see Jerusalem and the Tabernacle again he knew not. But he was so yielded up to God, he was so fully assured that *His* will was best, that even though it meant the loss of the throne and the loss of his life, he was content for Him to have His way—" let Him do to me as seemeth good unto Him."

There is no need to multiply examples, but a reflection upon the last case will be in place. If amid the shadows of the Old Testament dispensation, David was content for the Lord to have *His* way, now that the *heart* of God has been fully revealed at the Cross, how much more ought *we* to delight in the execution of His will! Surely we shall have no hesitation is saying—

> "*Ill* that *He* blesses is *our good*,
>   And *un*blest good is ill,
>   And all is right that seems most wrong,
>   If it be His sweet will."

8. It evokes a song of praise.

It could not be otherwise. Why should I, who am by nature no different from the careless and godless throngs all around, have been chosen in Christ before the foundation of the world and now blest with all spiritual blessings in the heavenlies in Him? Why was I, that once was an alien and a rebel, singled out for such wondrous favours? Ah, that is something I cannot fathom. Such grace, such love, " passeth knowledge." But if my mind is unable to discern a reason, my heart can express its gratitude in praise and adoration. But not only should I be grateful to God for His grace toward me in the past, His present dealings will fill me with thanksgivings. What is the force of that word, " *Rejoice in the Lord alway*" (Phil. 4 : 4)? Mark, it is not "Rejoice *in the Saviour*," but we are to "Rejoice in the Lord" *as* "Lord," as the *Master* of every circumstance. Need we remind the reader that when the apostle penned these words he was himself a prisoner in the hands of the Roman government. A long course of affliction and suffering lay behind him. Perils on land and perils on sea, hunger and thirst, scourging and stoning, had all been experienced. He had been persecuted by those within the church as well as by those without: the very ones who ought to have stood by him had forsaken him. And still he writes, " *Rejoice* in the

Lord *alway* "! What was the secret of his peace and happiness? Ah! had not this same apostle written, " And we know that all things *work together for good* to them that love God, to them who are the called according to His purpose " (Rom. 8: 28). But how did he, and how do we, " know," that *all* things work together for *good*? The answer is, Because *all things* are under the control of and are being regulated by the Supreme Sovereign, and because *He* has naught but thoughts of love toward His own, then " all things " are so ordered by Him that they are *made to minister to our ultimate good*. It is for this cause we are to give " thanks *always* for *all things* unto God and the Father in the name of our Lord Jesus Christ " (Eph. 5: 20). Yes, give thanks for " all things," for, as it has been well said, " Our disappointments are but *His* appointments." To the one who delights in the sovereignty of God the clouds not only have a " silver lining " but they are *silvern all through*, the darkness only serving to offset the light—

> "Ye fearful saints, fresh courage take;
> The clouds ye so much dread,
> Are *big with mercy* and shall break
> In blessings on your head."
>
> (WILLIAM COWPER)

9. IT GUARANTEES THE FINAL TRIUMPH OF GOOD OVER EVIL.

Ever since the day that Cain slew Abel, the conflict on earth between good and evil has been a sore problem to the saints. In every age the righteous have been hated and persecuted, whilst the unrighteous have appeared to defy God with impunity. The Lord's people, for the most part, have been poor in this world's goods, whereas the wicked in their temporal prosperity have flourished like the green bay tree. As one looks around and beholds the oppression of believers and the earthly success of unbelievers, and notes how few are the former and how numerous the latter; as he sees the apparent defeat of the right, and the triumphing of might and the wrong; as he hears the roar of battle, the cries of the wounded, and the lamentations of the bereaved; as he discovers that almost everything down here is in confusion, chaos, and ruins, it seems as though Satan were getting the better of the conflict. But as one looks *above*, instead of around, there is plainly visible to the eye of faith a Throne, a Throne unaffected by the storms of earth, a Throne that is " set," stable and secure; and upon it is seated One whose name is the Almighty, and who " worketh all things after the counsel of His own will " (Eph. 1 : 11). This then is our confidence—*God is on the Throne.* The helm is in *His* hand, and being Almighty, His purpose cannot fail, for " He is in one mind, and who can turn *Him?* and what His soul desireth, *even that He doeth* " (Job 23 : 13). Though God's governing hand is invisible to the eye of sense, it is real to faith, that faith which rests with sure confidence upon His Word, and therefore is assured *He cannot fail.* What follows below is from the pen of our brother Mr. Gaebelein.

" There can be no failure with God. ' God is not a man, that He should lie, neither the Son of man, that He should repent; hath He said and shall He not do it? or hath He spoken, and shall He not make it good?' (Num. 23 : 19). All will be accomplished. The promise made to His own beloved people to come for them and take them from hence to glory will not fail. He will surely come and gather them in His own presence. The solemn words spoken to the nations of the earth by the different prophets will also not fail. ' Come near, ye nations, to hear; and hearken ye people; let the earth hear, and all that is therein; the world, and all things that come forth of it. For the indignation of the Lord is upon all nations, and His fury upon all their armies; He hath utterly destroyed them, He hath delivered them to the slaughter ' (Isa. 34 : 1, 2). Nor will that day fail in which ' the lofty looks of man shall be humbled and the haughtiness of men shall be bowed down and the Lord alone shall be exalted ' (Isa. 2 : 11). The day in which He is manifested, when His glory shall cover the heavens, and His feet will stand again upon this earth, will surely come. His kingdom will not fail, nor all the promised events connected with the end of the age and the consummation.

THE VALUE OF THIS DOCTRINE

"In these dark and trying times how well it is to remember that He is on the throne, the throne which cannot be shaken, and that He will not fail in doing all He has spoken and promised. 'Seek ye out of the book of the Lord and read: Not one of these shall fail' (Isa. 34: 16). In believing, blessed anticipation, we can look on to the glory-time when His Word and His will is accomplished, when through the coming of the Prince of Peace, righteousness and peace comes at last. And while we wait for the supreme and blessed moment when His promise to us is accomplished, we trust Him, walking in His fellowship, and daily find afresh that He does not fail to sustain and keep us in all our ways."

10. It provides a resting-place for the heart.

Much that might have been said here has already been anticipated under previous heads. The One seated upon the Throne of Heaven, the One who is Governor over the nations and who has ordained and now regulates all events, is infinite not only in power but in wisdom and goodness as well. He who is Lord over all creations is the One that was "manifest in the flesh" (1 Tim. 3: 16). Ah! here is a theme no human pen can do justice to. The glory of God consists not merely in that He is Highest, but in that being high He stooped in lowly love to bear the burden of His own sinful creatures, for it is written "God was in Christ, reconciling the world unto Himself" (2 Cor. 5: 19). The Church of God was purchased "with His own Blood" (Acts 20: 28). It is upon the gracious self-humiliation of the King Himself that His kingdom is established. O wondrous Cross! By it He who suffered upon it has become not the Lord of our destinies (He was that before), but the Lord of our hearts. Therefore, it is not in abject terror that we bow before the Supreme Sovereign, but in adoring worship we cry, "Worthy is the Lamb that was slain to receive power, and riches, and wisdom, and strength, and honour, and glory, and blessing" (Rev. 5: 12).

Here then is the refutation of the wicked charge that *this* doctrine is a horrible calumny upon God and dangerous to

expound to His people. Can a doctrine be " horrible " and
" dangerous " that gives God His true place, that maintains
His rights, that magnifies His grace, that ascribes *all* glory to
Him and removes every ground of boasting from the creature? Can a doctrine be " horrible " and " dangerous "
which affords the saints a sense of security in danger, that
supplies them comfort in sorrow, that begets patience within
them in adversity, that evokes from them praise at all times?
Can a doctrine be " horrible " and " dangerous " which as-
sures us of the certain triumph of good over evil, and which
provides a sure resting-place for our hearts, and that place,
the perfections of the Sovereign Himself? No; a thousand
times, no. Instead of being " horrible and dangerous " *this*
doctrine of the Sovereignty of God is glorious and edifying,
and a due apprehension of it will but serve to make us exclaim with Moses, " *Who is like unto thee, O Lord, among
the gods?* who is like Thee, glorious in holiness, fearful in
praises, doing wonders?" (Ex. 15: 11).

CONCLUSION

"Alleluia: for the Lord God omnipotent reigneth" (Rev. 19:6).

WE turn now, in conclusion, to one or two of the difficulties commonly raised in connection with the Sovereignty of God. If God has not only pre-determined the salvation of His own, but has also fore-ordained the good works which they are to walk in (Eph. 2: 10), then what incentive remains for us to strive after practical godliness? If God has fixed the number of those who are to be saved, and the others are vessels of wrath fitted to destruction, then what encouragement have we to preach the Gospel to the lost? Let us take up these questions in the order of mention.

1. God's Sovereignty and the believer's growth in grace.

If God has fore-ordained everything that comes to pass, of what avail is it for *us* to "exercise" ourselves "unto godliness" (1 Tim. 4: 7)? If God has before ordained the good works in which we are to walk (Eph. 2: 10), then why should *we* be "careful to maintain good works" (Titus 3: 8)? This only raises once more the problem of human responsibility. Really, it should be enough for us to reply, God has *bidden* us do so. Nowhere does Scripture inculcate or encourage a spirit of fatalistic indifference. Contentment with our present attainments is expressly disallowed. The word to every believer is, "*Press* towards the mark for the prize of the high calling of God in Christ Jesus" (Phil. 3: 14). This was the apostle's aim, and it should be ours. Instead of hindering the development of Christian character, a proper apprehension and appreciation of God's sovereignty will forward it. Just as the sinner's *despair* of any help from himself is the first prerequisite of a sound conversion, so the loss of all confidence in himself is the first essential in the believer's growth in grace; and just as the sinner who despairs of help from himself will cast himself into the arms of sovereign mercy, so the Christian, conscious of his own frailty, will turn unto the Lord for power. It is when we are weak, we are strong (2 Cor. 12:10): that is to say, there must be *consciousness* of our weakness before we turn to the Lord for help. While the Christian allows the thought that he is sufficient in himself; while he imagines that by mere force of will he can resist temptation, while he has any confidence in the flesh; then, like Peter who *boasted* that though all forsook the Lord yet would not he, we shall certainly fail and fall. Apart from Christ we can do *nothing* (John 15:5). The promise of God is, " He giveth power to the faint; and *to them that have no might* (of their own) He increaseth strength " (Isa. 40:29).

The question now before us is of great practical importance, and we are deeply anxious to express ourselves clearly and simply. The secret of development of Christian character is the realization and acknowledgement of our own *powerlessness*, and the consequent turning unto the Lord for help. The plain fact is that of ourselves we are utterly unable to practise a single precept or obey a single command that is set before us in the Scriptures. For example: " Love your enemies "—but of ourselves we cannot do this, or make ourselves do it. " In nothing be anxious "—but who can avoid and prevent anxiety when things go wrong? These are merely examples selected at random from scores of others. Does then God *mock* us by bidding us do what He knows we are *unable* to do? The answer of Augustine to this question is the best we have met with—" God gives commands we cannot perform, that we may know *what* we ought to request from Him." A consciousness of our powerlessness should cast us upon Him who has all power. Here then is where a vision and view of God's sovereignty *helps*, for it reveals *His* sufficiency and shows us our *insufficiency*.

2. GOD'S SOVEREIGNTY AND CHRISTIAN SERVICE.

If God has determined before the foundation of the world

the precise number of those who shall be saved, then why should *we* concern ourselves about the eternal destiny of those with whom we come into contact? What place is left for *zeal* in Christian service? Will not the doctrine of God's sovereignty, and its corollary of predestination, *discourage* the Lord's servants from faithfulness in evangelism? No; instead of *dis*couraging His servants, a recognition of God's sovereignty is most *en*couraging to them. Here is one, for example, who is called upon to do the work of an evangelist, and he goes forth believing in the freedom of the will and in the sinner's own ability to come to Christ. He preaches the Gospel as faithfully and zealously as he knows how; but he finds the vast majority of his hearers are utterly indifferent and have no heart at all for Christ. He discovers that men are, for the most part, thoroughly wrapt up in the things of the world, and that few have any concern about the world to come. He beseeches men to be reconciled to God, and pleads with them over their soul's salvation. But it is of no avail. He becomes thoroughly disheartened, and asks himself, What is the use of it all? Shall he quit, or had he better change his mission and message? If men will not respond to the Gospel, had he not better engage in that which is more popular and acceptable to the world? Why not occupy himself with humanitarian efforts, with social-uplift work, with the purity campaign? Alas! that so many men who once preached the Gospel are now engaged in these activities instead.

What then is God's corrective for His discouraged servant? First, he needs to learn from Scripture that God is not now seeking to convert the world, but that in this Age He is " taking out of the Gentiles " a people for His name (Acts 15: 14). What then is God's corrective for His discouraged servant? This—a proper apprehension of *God's* plan for this dispensation. Again: what is God's remedy for dejection at apparent failure in our labours? This—the assurance that *God's* purpose *cannot* fail, that God's plans *cannot* miscarry, that God's will *must* be done. *Our* labours are not intended to bring about that which *God* has not decreed. Once more:

what is God's word of cheer for the one who is thoroughly disheartened at the lack of response to his appeals and the absence of fruit for his labours? This—that *we* are not responsible for results: that is *God's* side, and *God's* business. Paul may " plant," and Apollos may " water," but it is *God* who " gave the increase " (1 Cor. 3:6). Our business is to obey Christ and preach the Gospel to every creature, to emphasize the " Whosoever believeth," and then to leave the Holy Spirit to apply the Word in quickening power to whom He wills, resting on the sure promise of Jehovah—" For as the rain cometh down, and the snow from heaven, and returneth not thither, but watereth the earth, and maketh it bring forth and bud, that it may give seed to the sower, and bread to the eater: So shall My Word be that goeth forth out of My mouth: *it shall not return unto Me void,* but it shall accomplish *that which I please* [it may not accomplish that which *we* please], and it shall prosper in the thing *whereto I sent it* " (Isa. 55:10, 11). Was it not this assurance that sustained the beloved apostle when he declared " Therefore I endure all things *for the elect's sake* " (2 Tim. 2:10)! Yea, is not this same lesson to be learned from the blessed example of the Lord Jesus! When we read that He said to the people, " Ye also have seen Me, and *believe not*," He fell back upon the sovereign pleasure of the One who sent Him, saying, " *All* that the Father giveth Me *shall* come to Me, and him that cometh to Me I will in no wise cast out " (John 6:36, 37). He knew that His labour would not be in vain. He knew God's Word would not return unto Him " void." He knew that " God's elect " *would* come to Him and believe Him. And this same assurance fills the soul of every servant who intelligently rests upon the blessed truth of God's sovereignty.

Ah fellow-Christian-worker, God has not sent us forth to " draw a bow at a venture." The success of the ministry which He has committed into our hands is not left contingent on the fickleness of the wills of those to whom we preach. How gloriously encouraging and soul-sustaining are those words of our Lord's, if we rest on them in simple faith:

" And other sheep I have [" have," mark you, *not* " will have"; "have," because given to Him by the Father before the foundation of the world], which are not of this fold (i.e. the Jewish fold then existing): them also I *must* bring, and they *shall* hear My voice " (John 10: 16). Not simply, " they *ought* to hear My voice," not simply " they *may* hear My voice," not " they will do so *if* they are willing." There is no " if," no " perhaps," no uncertainty about it. " They *shall* hear My voice " is His own positive, unqualified, absolute promise. Here then, is where *faith* is to rest! Continue your quest, dear friend, after the " other sheep " of Christ's. Be not discouraged because the " goats " heed not His voice as you preach the Gospel. Be faithful, be scriptural, be persevering, and Christ may use even you to be His mouthpiece in calling some of His lost sheep unto Himself. " Therefore, my beloved brethren, be ye stedfast, unmoveable, always abounding in the work of the Lord, forasmuch as ye *know* that your labour is *not in vain* in the Lord " (1 Cor. 15: 58).

It now remains for us to offer a few closing reflections and our happy task is finished.

God's sovereign election of certain ones to salvation is a MERCIFUL provision. The sufficient answer to all the wicked accusations that the doctrine of Predestination is cruel, horrible, and unjust, is that, *unless* God had chosen certain ones to salvation, *none* would have been saved, for " there is none that seeketh after God " (Rom. 3: 11). This is no mere inference of ours but the definite teaching of Holy Scripture. Attend closely to the words of the apostle in Romans 9, where this theme is fully discussed—" Though the number of the children of Israel be as the sand of the sea, *a remnant* shall be saved.... And as Isaiah said before, *Except* the Lord of hosts *had left us a seed*, we had been as Sodom, *and been made like unto Gomorrah* " (Rom. 9: 27, 29). The teaching of this passage is unmistakable: but for Divine interference, Israel would have become as Sodom and Gomorrah. Had God left Israel alone, human depravity would have run its course to its own tragic end. But God left Israel a " remnant " or " seed." Of old the cities of the plain had been obliterated for their sin, and none was left to survive them; and so it would have been in Israel's case had not God " left " or spared a remnant. Thus it is with the human race: but for God's sovereign grace in sparing a remnant, *all* of Adam's descendants had perished in their sins. Therefore, we say that God's sovereign election of certain ones to salvation is a *merciful* provision. And, be it noted, in choosing the ones He did, God did no *injustice* to the others who were passed by, for *none* had any *right* to salvation. Salvation is by *grace*, and the *exercise* of grace is a matter of pure *sovereignty*—God might save all or none, many or few, one or ten thousand, just as He saw best. Should it be replied, But surely it were " best " to save *all*. The answer would be: *We* are not capable of judging. *We* might have thought it " best " if God had never created Satan, never allowed sin to enter the world, or sin having entered, if He had brought the conflict between good and evil to an end long before now. Ah! God's ways are not ours, and His ways are " past finding out."

God fore-ordains everything which comes to pass. His sovereign rule extends throughout the entire Universe and is over every creature. " For *of* Him, and *through* Him, and *to* Him, are *all things*" (Rom. 11: 36). God initiates all things, regulates all things, and all things are working unto His eternal glory. " There is but one God, the Father, *of whom are all things,* and we in Him; and one Lord Jesus Christ, *by whom are all things,* and we by Him " (1 Cor. 8: 6). And again, " According to the purpose of Him who *worketh all things after the counsel of His own will* " (Eph. 1: 11). Surely, if anything can be ascribed to *chance*, it is the *drawing of lots*, and yet the Word of God expressly declares, " The lot is cast into the lap; *but the whole disposing thereof is of the Lord* " (Prov. 16: 33)!

God's wisdom in the government of our world shall yet be completely vindicated before all created intelligences. God is no idle Spectator, looking on from a distant world at the happenings on our earth, but is Himself shaping everything to the ultimate promotion of His own glory. Even now He is working out His eternal purpose, not only in spite of human and Satanic opposition, but by means of them. How wicked and futile have been all efforts to resist His will shall one day be as fully evident as when of old He overthrew the rebellious Pharaoh and his hosts at the Red Sea.

It has been well said, " The end and object of all is the glory of God. It is perfectly, divinely true, that ' God hath ordained for His own glory whatsoever comes to pass.' In order to guard this from all possibility of mistake, we have only to remember who is this God, and what the glory that He seeks. It is He who is the God and Father of our Lord Jesus Christ—of Him in whom divine love came seeking *not* her own, and who was among us as ' One that serveth.' It is He who, sufficient in Himself, can receive no real accession of glory from His creatures, but from whom cometh down every good and every perfect gift, in whom is no variableness nor shadow of turning. Of His own alone can His creatures give to Him."

" The glory of such an one is found in the display of His own goodness, righteousness, holiness, truth; in manifesting Himself as in Christ He has manifested Himself and will for-ever. The glory of this God is what of necessity *all things must serve*—adversaries and evil as well as all else. *He has ordained it*; His power will ensure it; and when all apparent clouds and obstructions are removed, then shall He rest— ' rest in His love ' for ever, although eternity only will suffice for the apprehension of the revelation. ' *God shall be all in all* ' gives in six words the ineffable result." (F. W. Grant on " Atonement," our italics.)

What we have written gives but an incomplete and imperfect presentation of this most important subject, we must sorrowfully confess. Nevertheless, if it results in a clearer apprehension of the majesty of God and His sovereign mercy, we shall be amply repaid for our labours. If the reader *has* received blessing from the perusal of these pages, let him not fail to return thanks to the Giver of every good and every perfect thing, ascribing all praise to His inimitable and sovereign grace.

> "Great God! how infinite art Thou,
> What weak and worthless worms are we,
> Let all the race of creatures bow
> And seek salvation now from Thee.
> Eternity, with all its years
> Stands ever-present to Thy view,
> To Thee there's nothing old appears.
> Great God! there can be nothing new.
> Our lives through varied scenes are drawn,
> And vexed with mean and trifling cares;
> While Thine eternal thought moves on
> Thy fixed and undisturbed affairs."

"*Alleluia: for the Lord God omnipotent reigneth*" (Rev. 19:6).

SOME OTHER
BANNER OF TRUTH TRUST
PUBLICATIONS

PROFITING FROM THE WORD

A. W. PINK

How much profit do we gain from our reading of the Bible? 'All Scripture', we are told in 2 Timothy 3: 16, 17, 'is profitable', but how much do we gain from our reading of Scripture, and by what means can we learn to profit more?

These questions, which are so fundamental to Christian experience and happiness, provide the theme for this new book by Arthur Pink. Originally published as a series in *Studies in the Scripture*, a monthly magazine edited by the author for over 30 years, it has all the characteristics which have, since the author's death in 1952, led to his recognition as one of the finest Christian writers of the twentieth century. Certainly the present book is among his best and will be a help to Christians both young and old.

Paperback 144 *pp*

THE PURITAN HOPE

Revival and the Interpretation of Prophecy

IAIN MURRAY

'With whole-hearted commitment to the plenary inspiration of the Scriptures Iain Murray argues with exegetical competence and fairness for the position of world-wide revival in history before the Second Advent of Christ. This is the Puritan Hope. It involves the conversion of Gentile multitudes and the certain prospect of the national conversion of the Jews, apart from a reign of Christ on earth, which is based on a careful exegesis of Old Testament prophecy and Romans eleven. The means for this accomplishment will be by the preaching of the gospel of sovereign grace and the powerful operations of the Spirit of God. The author envisages objections to this view by millenarians and answers cogently. In the present sad state of the Christian Church this book should prove to be a tonic ...'

David Freeman The Westminster Theological Journal

'Perhaps the most important practical aspect of this study is its demonstration of the influence which the "Puritan Hope" had on the beginnings of the modern missionary movement. Carey and others, who attempted great things for God because they expected great things from God, were far from giving any place in their thoughts to that pessimism over the future of the Church's work in the world which here and there, in more recent generations, has acquired the status of a new orthodoxy. ... Mr. Murray has written a book of high importance, which deserves to be studied and pondered by evangelical christians.'

F. F. Bruce The Life of Faith

Paperback, illustrated, 328 pp

RIGHT WITH GOD

JOHN BLANCHARD

Some people know what Christianity is and reject it. More do not know and do not wish to know. But there are many who belong to neither of these classes. They do not reject; they are not indifferent; yet they have not found a personal knowledge of God. It is to help those who thus search that this book has been written.

The author's first concern is to remove the main cause of spiritual uncertainty, namely, ignorance of what the Bible teaches. What this teaching is, as it concerns our individual relation to God, is set out clearly, step by step. And it leads positively to the Bible's own conclusion, that salvation is free and undeserved and received through the work of Jesus Christ, the Son of God. 'For God sent not his Son into the world to condemn the world; but that the world through him might be saved.'

John Blanchard was born in Guernsey in the Channel Islands in 1932. After thirteen years in the Guernsey Civil Service he has since 1965 been wholly engaged in a ministry of evangelism and Bible teaching with the Movement for World Evangelization. *Right With God*, first published in 1971, is now in its sixth printing, having sold widely throughout the English-speaking world. It has been translated into French, German, Italian, Spanish, Greek, Japanese, Portuguese and Sinhalese, and is issued in Braille by Torch Trust for the Blind, and on tape by Tape-Aids for the Blind (South Africa).

Paperback 128 *pp*